MW01234667

BREEDING LEAH

and Other Stories

. . . .

BREEDING LEAH
and Other Stories

John Bennion

Signature Books Salt Lake City 1991

. . . .

For my father near Kolob

"Dust" was first published in *Ascent* 14 (1988), 1:1-10, and reprinted in *Best of the West II* (Layton, UT: Gibbs Smith, 1989), 120-34.

"Breeding Leah" was first published in *Utah Holiday*, Dec. 1989, 46-50.

"The Interview" was first published in *Dialogue: A Journal of Mormon Thought* 18 (Summer 1985): 167-76.

"A Court of Love" was first published in *Sunstone* 12 (1988), 2:30-38.

"A House of Order" was first published in *Dialogue: A Journal of Mormon Thought* 21 (Fall 1988): 129-48.

AUTHOR'S NOTE: All characters in this work of fiction are the products of my imagination. Any resemblance to actual people is accidental.

COVER ILLUSTRATION: CAROL NORBY, COLLAGE, 1991
COVER DESIGN: LARRY CLARKSON

Composed and printed in the United States of America

95   94   93   92   91   6   5   4   3   2   1

LIBRARY OF CONGRESS CATALOGING-IN-PUBLICATION DATA
Bennion, John, 1953–
    Breeding Leah and other stories / John Bennion.
    Contents: Dust — Breeding Leah — The interview — A court of love — A house
of order — The last wonder of nature — Jenny, captured by the Mormons.
    ISBN 0-941214-94-X : $14.95
    I. Title.
PS3552.E547564B74   1991
813'.54—dc20   91-22693
                                                                          CIP

CONTENTS

dụ̈s̈ṭ

Dry Springs, Utah: My Father's Property. Since morning my eye has inclined toward the road below my cabin, perhaps because today marks the second anniversary of my removal to the desert. I'm expecting no one in particular, but the wavering, ground-heated air gives the alkali flat the appearance of movement as if a cloud of white dust billows from its surface. Such a cloud could signify either an approaching vehicle or a misdirected shell, a gift from the chemical weapons testing facility north of here. My polygamist neighbors to the south might read the coil of dust as a sign of the Apocalypse. Leaving my window, I walk three hundred steps to the butte behind my cabin, halfway between Salt Lake City and Ely, Nevada.

Like the uncertain cloud, the butte presents diverse aspects: breast-shaped but with a column of lava on top, an igneous plug which my eye reads as either the thick phallus of the volcano's last thrust or as a hardened black nipple. From this vantage I inspect for any change in the size or direction of the potential cloud. The white blotch shimmers in the heat, dust motes whirling, as real as the pillar of fire in De Mille's *Ten Commandments*.

Rockwood, Utah: Forty Miles Northeast. From my position I can see the range of mountains around my former home. My wife, Sylvia, and our five children—Benjamin, Abigail, Joshua, Ruth, and Heather—live there with my mother in the town named after my violent great-grandfather, James Darren Rockwood, who was once a body-guard to the Mormon prophet Joseph Smith. Some historians claim that Great-grandpa shot the mayor of Carthage, Illinois, Frederick Diggs, because Diggs harassed the People of God. Grandpa J. D.'s violence is genetic: my brother poisoned his boss after being fired, and I experienced a sign of religious fulfillment after completing the chemical blueprint for the nerve gas that killed the sheep.

In Rockwood when I changed my daughter's diapers, she raised her arms above her head so I could tickle her. "Doat," she said. "Doat, Daddy." Her laugh comes from her belly, a gurgle of mirth. The faces of my wife and older son were identically solemn when I left them two years ago.

Alone on my inherited section of desert, I try to isolate my fear of the Apocalypse, but the core of my fear is as various as the cloud of dust.

Skull Valley Testing Grounds: The Limits of Non-radioactive Gas. Formerly I worked thirty miles to the northwest of here, where the government designs, tests, and stores lesser tools of the Apocalypse. To approach my bunker I passed through three barriers—woven wire, chain link, brick—presenting my I.D. to three sets of guards. My fingerprints were taken daily to insure that the guards, who saw me daily, hadn't mistaken my face.

As head chemist my duty was to create equations on a blackboard. Two second-level chemists transferred the numbers and letters to paper, a committee ordered the batch, and technicians, dozens of them, manipulated the stuff with long-armed machinery from behind thick glass windows. Working over my abstractions, I was elevated to a pure sphere, like a high priest delineating the mind of God.

Once on my way home from work, a great ball of orange gas flung outward from one of the army's testing bunkers, boiling toward my car past the boundary fence. I shit myself, understanding that the mind of God held subtleties I hadn't yet grasped. I didn't breathe while I bounced across the desert road for three miles. Behind me the wind gathered the potent molecules, dissipating them upward toward the bench land of the nearby mountains.

The newspapers soon discovered that five thousand head of Hyrum Jorgenson's sheep had died. Government veterinarians explained that the animals were undernourished and had eaten loco weed. Within a year two movies were made about the event: *Rage*, starring George C. Scott, whose son was killed by the descending gas, and *Whiffs*, a spoof which showed tendrils of white drifting through nearby Tooele, Utah. The excitement of seeing their children as extras caused all my friends to forget the dead sheep. After viewing both movies, I had the recurring dream that a technician found a way to disseminate my gas using an atomic warhead.

The summer of our first wedding anniversary, my water turn came between one and three in the morning. Several times Sylvia crept down through the cedars above our horse pasture, wrapped only in a blanket, and seduced me before I could remove my irrigation boots.

Lot's Wife: Does Flesh Turn to Sodium Inside Ground Zero? The morning after my bolt of terror, a Saturday, Sylvia and I lay in bed late. The children played in the next room, waiting for breakfast. "That's Daddy's briefcase," Benjamin said. "He won't like you playing with it."

"He won't mind," Ruth said. "He won't mind at all."

"He will."

"Daddy, Daddy, Daddy," the baby said into the shut door. Sylvia smiled but I couldn't: the word didn't seem to apply to me. We

3

heard struggling and a shower of papers. Then I smiled. I didn't go to work the next Monday.

After the third month without a paycheck, Sylvia began to think my fears were silly. "You've got to face it that accidents happen." She shouted arguments at me. I shouted my fear back. Abigail started taking long walks. The baby crawled into our bed every night, unable to sleep alone. Finally, insecure myself, I spanked her to make her stay in her own bed. Joshua wet his pants three days out of five at school. "I try to make it to the toilet, but I can't get there in time," he said. Their troubles, poignant as they were, had little to do with me. I told Sylvia I was going to live on my father's property in the desert.

"Dramatic," she said. "It's really just Andrea, isn't it? You're going to pretend you're pioneering with her." Hungry for land, my father had homesteaded farther and farther west; he finally abandoned my mother, who wouldn't leave Salt Lake City to live in the desert with him. I couldn't understand either my father's motivating dream or the adulterous one Sylvia supplied for me.

When she plays the guitar, Sylvia sits in her rocking chair, eyes closed. Her fingers ripple on the strings, moving according to laws of clarity, grace, and intuition, marked by the rhythm of the moving chair.

An Acolyte's Guide to Androgynous Thinking. On this, the second anniversary of leaving my job, my town, and my family, I don't trust my eye's interest in the cloud of dust. My mental/ emotional apparatus will take any non-event today and say, "This is what you were waiting for. The reverberation of the coming event impinged on your neurons, causing the condition you call anticipation." I say to my neurons, "Parascience." I deny that my brain picks up invisible signals and creates an impossible tension between me and some other object in time or space. Despite my lack of faith in my own nervous system, my flesh still organizes itself for someone's possible arrival. And I'm double-minded again, split between rationality and mysticism, unable to be either a scientist or a saint, as if the bolt of fear at the swarming gas traumatized my corpus callosum, the bridge in my brain.

Coriantumr, Utah. Five miles south of my cabin lives a community of apostates from the Mormon church, two hundred strong, who have returned to the practices of the nineteenth-century pioneers—living in polygamy with all things in common. In preparation for the last day, they have hoarded wheat, honey, and rifles. To satisfy present needs they have a Montessori school and a dairy. They sent a group of their brethren to Switzerland to purchase a strain of bacteria for culturing milk into cheese which they trade in Paradise, farther south. They want to pipe the water from my spring to their alfalfa fields so they can grow feed for another fifty cows, but they never mention that. A hundred miles southwest of them lies Ely, where madames and casino owners also live with everything in common.

A Star Named Kolob. My father, the former owner of this property, is in heaven, which the polygamists have determined to be on a planet near the star Kolob, a hundred trillion miles past our sun.God lives there, they believe, with all the spirits who are waiting to come to earth. My sixth through twelfth children are presently on Kolob also, they say. I doubt that my wife's rhythm and my own will coincide seven more times, but that doesn't concern the polygamists.

A Six-by-four Patch of Floor Under My Chalkboard: Vive Vas Deferens. During lunch in my bunker at Skull Valley Testing Grounds, I ate tomato sandwiches, the juice running down my fingers onto the floor. My co-chemist, Andrea Armstrong, looked at me across my red and dripping hands. Suddenly we were tumbling on the floor in the chalk dust and sandwich remains. Upon confessing this to my Mormon bishop, I was disfellowshipped from the church. My lack of guilt disgusted him; my emotional incontinence worried me.

Salt Lake City, Utah: A Hundred Miles Northeast of Rockwood. On the highest spire of the temple the gold statue of Moroni, his horn to his lips, prepares to signal the rolling together of the scroll.

5

Sometimes in my dreams I hear his trump and then sense the stealthy movement of the quivering gas.

My Journal: The Tao of Listing. Like Robinson Crusoe I have a "certain Stupidity of Soul" and like him I trust lists, not of provisions, but of anchors in space and time. Lists are beautiful—they don't whine. They require no explanation, are non-ardent, non-causal, calm, static, unpretentious, a periodic table of my own elements. However I'm wary of listing *toward*, as in "Our ship listed toward starboard after it struck the rock" or "Since morning my eye has listed toward the junction."

A selection from Robinson Crusoe's list:

>small Ropes and Rope-twine
>a Piece of spare Canvass
>a barrel of wet Gunpowder
>a great Hogshead of Bread
>three large Runlets of Rum or Spirits
>a Box of Sugar

My list:

>the black ridge extending between here and Ely, Nevada, looking like God's darkening brow
>the bank of the spring my father cleared out twenty-five years ago
>the pattern of tomato seeds on Andrea's back
>my son skipping rocks across a green pond
>the harmony of equations across the blackboard, the purer image of the orange gas
>the Rorschach blots created in a mobile cloud

Andrea, Kolob, and I: The Physics of Attraction Between Bodies. Sitting on the butte with the border of Nevada a wall behind me, I can sense the faint reverberations of these places and events. Closing my eyes, I sense here the great salt sea, here the mounds of stored bombs and gasses, here my wife and children, my friends, Kolob, the potential cloud, the polygamists. I feel the lines of tension—physical, disinterested—between myself and them.

The Angle of the Cloud: Playing the Futures. If the dust materializes from the north today, it may be Sergeant Mertzke, recreation administrator for the officers' club at Skull Valley Testing Grounds. He was once a hunting buddy of my father and me, but when I see his dust, I'll compose myself, adopting a persona which will fit into his consciousness — either the cautious, land-loving son of my father or the chemist who strained after one too many formulae.

"Have they left?" he says, referring to the deer he wants to shoot by spotlight from the back of his jeep.

"A five-point, two spikes, six doe." I count on my fingers.

"Where're you going to get a better offer?" And he explains again the idea of an R&R area. He looks over this desert property, barren except for the fifty square yards around the spring, and sees officers and women of the New Army frolicking through the sagebrush.

"I don't know," I say. "Land's stable, money's mobile."

"But gauge the possibilities."

I won't disturb his vision of my father's property, but before he gets to the part about the raw hunters returning to the tents of their women, I will recast myself as the religious ascetic — a desert saint. I motion for silence, bowing my head. "I will ask." Holding him with my silence for five, maybe ten minutes. "No. My father near Kolob says no. He warns you that God is as displeased with you as he was with the people of Sodom and Gomorrah. His wrath is kindled."

"The hell it is," he says. He comes in the evening despite my warning, the fever for killing heavy in him. I flash the spotlight on this doe, that buck. He shoots and I hear the thud as his hollow-points hit muscle and bone. Even the shower of blood creates no motion inside of me. I could be butcher, conservationist, harvester, accomplice. Any of these could explain my relationship to the event: the spurting blood. Nothing moves.

On winter mornings my son built elaborate houses out of chairs, blankets, boards, and cushions. Once he and his siblings decided that the structure was a houseboat and that I was the shark. My baby lifted her body onto her toes, pumping her legs in place as she tried to escape. I ate her squealing body four times.

The Ark: How Many Roentgens Will Kill a Dove? If the dust arrives from the south, it will come slowly: three of the brethren from the polygamous camp navigating the ruts and rocks in their decrepit pickup.

"Brother Rockwood," the Elders say. "Toward the end of the world, wars and pestilence will be poured out upon the land. The moon will turn red like blood, and lightning will flash from the east to the west as the Son of Man approaches. Only the righteous — those who have entered the new order — will be spared."

I lead them along. "Vanity, vanity," I say. "The work of man's own hands will destroy the world. The only thing that will spare any of us is your buried vault."

"The mind of God moves in mysterious ways."

They have a stainless steel and cement ark buried fifty feet under the desert. Its walls are six feet thick. They plan to go down there and emerge two by two, or rather one by seven, into the Millennium. I could believe their myth that the Pentagon, public education, and the mind of Satan move in collusion toward the Apocalypse, but I don't let myself trust major abstractions anymore. At this point I profane the name of their God and deny their pragmatic mysticism. "I am a rational, enlightened humanist," I say. "A member of a powerful conspiracy." And they leave saddened because I can't comprehend their God or their milk barn.

Masters and Johnson on Solitude: Why Crusoe Kept Goats. Through a pleasant inversion of perspective, for a moment the potential dust is my own as I drive my white Ford Fairlane southward to Ely for the weekly venting of my seminal vesicles. In the back are stacks of *Chemical Review*, a weight which keeps me from getting stuck when it's winter. As I drive I call myself adulterer, hedonist, lecher, fallen saint: but all the fragments crumble before I can build them into a consistent foundation. I drive quickly past the polygamist town made of two-story houses large as dormitories. Beyond their community the volcanic ridge resurfaces, connecting me with Ely.

I park my car in the city and shuffle toward a casino under the swirl of lights. For the girls and the card dealers, I am the rich and eccentric desert rat, dusty, hunch-shouldered. I engage the first prostitute I see, a sad-eyed woman with long black hair. In our room she takes off her clothing slowly. The absurdity of our puny climax drains the life from me, and I feel disconnected. However, she is efficient, improvising with clever lips and tongue, and she makes my body perform. I spend the rest of the evening flipping the lever of a slot machine, anticipating a windfall.

The Prodigal Father. A northern originating dust could also signify my friend, Jonathan Boone, driving from Rockwood. "Howard, your wife is pining," he says. "She's got no money. She's getting food and clothing from the Bishop's Storehouse and that makes her ashamed. What can I tell her? Is what you're doing worth the problems you're causing?"

"I'm making no stand," I say to him.

"Why do you stay here?"

"I've got no reform in mind," I say.

"Just come back with me."

"Please don't talk anymore," I ask him. He doesn't understand the ways his questions strain my introspective faculty. For an hour we walk in the cool of the evening. The breeze has died and, bending low, we smell the mint growing on the banks of my spring.

Options on My Father's Property. If I wait long enough, my back against the butte, someone comes. Last week a friend who was a Democratic Socialist in college drove through. Still an idealist after twenty years, he looked around, and his vision was powerful enough to transform the dead soil.

"This is like paradise," he said.

"No, that's twenty miles farther on."

"Can you picture a community here, all friends, lovers, family? People who have repudiated hate." His voice nearly revived my own dreams of Zion, a place where people live in peace. "We could cast off the dead husk of society," he said, and I understood he wanted to build a nudist retreat.

"I won't sell."

"I don't want you to sell." He was eager, running through the greasewood and shadscale, blinded by his narrow optimism, believing that, along with their socks and underwear, people can discard their impulse to aggression.

For him I was the sharp agribusinessman. "My god. This land can produce seven maybe eight tons of prime alfalfa to the acre, and you talk to me about a damn spa. That spring brings up two or three feet of water per second, and all you can think of is some kind of orgy." He left in his jeep, driving with only a centimeter of metal between him and the sky.

The Penultimate Human. Once a man drove through looking for the road to Topaz Mountain. He had his wife and children with him — a family man on an outing. He showed me a sample of a geode he'd found. "We cut and polish these nippers. A real fine hobby for the kids, and it teaches them something. Might as well kill two birds with one stone." He laughed, watching for my response. "Every second they're polishing, they're learning geology. And then we sell them. Isn't it something? A real tidy income." The pleasant wife and children smiled and nodded.

His soft-bellied words irritated me, violated my integrity. I told him the blacktop began twenty miles farther. If the heat is great enough when the lightning flashes from east to west, his stones will melt to glass. For him my eyes became hard and clear, glistening with intensity. "Gog and Magog are gathering for battle: the Apocalypse draws near," I said. "I-Am-That-I-Am says 'Beware the wrath of the Lamb.'" Wide-eyed, he left me alone to ruminate on my father's property.

Personal History: An Escape From My True Self Before God. I can establish no relationship with any point or person secondary to myself in space which is as important as my fear. No end depends from a middle in my life, no new and glorious future grows organically out of my past, as Aristotle, Alexander Hamilton, Walt Whitman, Brigham Young, Horatio Alger, and Karl Marx promised.

When my son was two he backed into a kettle we had set for scalding chickens. I tore off his diaper and turned the hose full across him. His back and buttocks peeled white wherever the water touched. Later he clawed the healing skin, biting my hands when I held his. I slapped his mouth, hard, and the print faded slowly.

When he was three he helped me harvest corn from our garden, pulling the sheath downward from the silk, breaking out the yellow ears. We filled ten buckets with corn for bottling.

When I was four I walked across this property, following my father as he planned where the fences would go on his new homestead—640 acres of desert land. He bought a faded red diesel engine to pump water from the slow-flowing spring.

I was six. My father sent me to this cabin from the fields a mile eastward, where he was working. "You start dinner," he said. "I'll be along." The road I watched back over became dark through the window. The coyotes yelping made the loneliest sound I have ever heard. He didn't come until an hour after the food was cold.

For years from behind our kitchen door in Rockwood, I heard my mother and father arguing religion: evolution, modern revelation, Christ's miracles, Joseph Smith talking to God. "If the prophet in Salt Lake told you to walk off a cliff, you would do it, wouldn't you?" my father said.

"But he wouldn't ask," said my mother.

"But if he did?"

"But he won't."

Once I fell asleep while listening, and my father discovered me, from my snoring he said, and carried me to my bed.

When I was nine I cut out the heart of a newly dead rattlesnake and watched it beat eighty-three times in the palm of my hand. During my seventeenth summer as my friend and I irrigated the farm, we grew a potato plant which we watered with only our urine.

When I was twenty-two and Sylvia wouldn't see me any more, my father rode on horseback with me over the mountains surrounding Rockwood and down into the desert toward this homestead. Each night he talked to me about his life, telling me stories, singing songs to me his mother had sung to him — administering to my pain with his voice. Sometimes now I hear him murmuring to me out of the rocks above my cabin.

In 1973 when diesel prices started rising with gasoline prices and he couldn't afford to pump water from the spring anymore, my father sold the ranch on mortgage and repossessed it four times: from some dairy farmers out of central Utah, from a group of Salt Lake bankers, from a machinist who wanted to live in the desert with his family, and from a sheepman who wanted to build sheds for his herds. None of them could make the property produce.

One year before my father died, the day we finished hauling our second crop of hay, I drove him to the shack someone built over a mineral pool ten miles west of here. His mind was already partly in the next world, and he howled and swore as I lugged him into the water, which was heavy as amniotic fluid. I guess he thought I would scald him. I only wanted to ease his joints, but I howled with him as we floated.

When I was thirty my father imagined that the sighing of the wind through the boulders was Marilyn Monroe and her sirens, who had inhabited the butte. He renamed it Whorehouse Rock in her honor. One night he climbed naked through the snow to visit her. When we found him near where I'm sitting, coyotes had gnawed his nose, ears, and penis.

In the genealogical library in Salt Lake City, I tried to trace my ancestry back to Adam. Once I discovered their names and dates of birth, temple officiators could seal each family member to me by ordinance, soul by soul creating an eternal indivisible unity. As I worked I felt a completeness-in-others: I was the epiphany toward which all those souls had been living. In my research I only made it back to 1698 to a man who had to run away from Wales because he murdered his landlord.

When Abigail was small she squirted steaming sauce on the back of her hand while eating a Sloppy Joe. I placed a leaf of iceberg lettuce on the burn to draw the heat out. She ate the rest of the meal with one hand, balancing the green leaf on her other fist.

The Broken Flask. I have more fragments of my own history, but if I add them point-by-point, measuring the degree of gravity between each one, what is their sum? — a minute and irrepressible motion of my chromosomes toward the Apocalypse. From whom can I learn how to think about this singular and revolutionary inclination?

Can I sacrifice my wife and children to warn the people as Abraham and Tolstoy did? Can I like Moses carry myself and my children toward a new world after the fire storms and plagues? Like Einstein or Newton can I invent a new mathematics, a tool for analyzing my inscrutable impulse toward destruction? The prophet of the polygamists and a Navaho Indian I once knew both believed that they could make it rain by thinking. Can I like Kierkegaard concentrate so fully, a Knight of vital Faith, that mental impulses become corporeal and I purge this violence from my blood? I can find no myth, no introspective process, through which I can reconnect myself to my father, my wife, or my children: a double-minded man is uncertain in all his ways. I am here, not farming my father's property, while my autobiography unravels itself.

On good days, after someone leaves, it is only me independent — no frustrated motion. No pointing finger or angle of apprehension. During those minutes I float in benevolent stasis, a calm which is always violated by my anticipation. As of this moment I repudiate the road from which dust does not yet rise. The iron-gray igneous rocks dribbled out over the land in confusion, the ashen alkali desert: these are the emblems of my new world, the world which waits for the cloud.

As I leave the butte behind my cabin, I make an oath that I will hold myself firm against returning to watch again. I will not picture her face and the firm line along her jaw as she drives across the desert—four children in the back of the car, one in the front. The children sit with their hands on their knees, and they say nothing though the air inside the car is stifling.

BREEDING

Leah

Through the bulk of the winter Carl and Amanda lived on oatmeal, potatoes, and turkey legs: policy in the psych department held that financial hardship weeded out weak graduate assistants. Then Amanda miscarried and became sick enough that she quit her classes and lost both her scholarship money and the day care that the university provided for her two children. Finally their fortunes changed, and Carl found a second job moving irrigation pipes on a farm in Erda, thirty miles southwest of Salt Lake. Carl's only agricultural experience had come from a month spent on his grandfather's farm when he was twelve, but the owner, whose main operation was in Colorado, assured him that was sufficient.

"We have to leave the city?" asked Amanda.

"Where else can *either* of us work for only seven hours a week and pay for rent and groceries." The owner had shown Carl a trim, white house with a large garden and with pens which they could fill with animals for eating.

"Wait'll Mother hears we're going to live off the land," said

Amanda. Since she had felt well enough to work, she had been unable to find a job which paid much more than day-care for C. J.
and Sammy. "She warned me we'd sink to this." Carl winced; his
mother-in-law called him a "visionary rustic"—an uncomfortable
label for a city-dwelling behaviorist.

"How does that feel?" he said their third night on the farm.
(He had thrown his leg across hers and began rubbing his palm
across her back.)

"What's on your mind?" she asked.

Through the open window Carl heard the tap-tapping of the
nozzles on the irrigation pipes and breathed the moist vapor, the
aroma of wheat and alfalfa greening. He also smelled another
kind of fecundity, the dry odor of manure decomposing in the
barnyard. He thought of feeding animals and then shoveling
their rich dust into his garden—participating intimately in the cycles of nature. "What do you *think* is on my mind?" he said, his
voice sly.

"You can't fool me. You're trying to butter me up." She smiled,
waiting. For some time Carl had been working to persuade her that
they should have another child.

"Pigs."

"What?" She sat up in bed.

"I want to raise pigs."

"No."

"I've considered it carefully."

"No." She rolled away. "No, no, no."

"I helped on my grand—"

"So a month makes you an expert," she said to the wall.

Carl switched on the lamp and pulled several pamphlets from
under the bed. The pictures displayed fat sows in pens with piglets
all around. "Look at the figures." Reaching across her shoulder, he
held a clipping from a newspaper in front of her face. It said "Hog
Futures" and Amanda wouldn't touch it. "At least consider how
much we can make. Ten sows gestate for four months. They each

have ten piglets, bringing thirty dollars apiece. Two cycles a year makes six thousand dollars, gross."

"You haven't included what they'll eat."

"I estimate less than a thousand dollars of feed a year."

"We can't even feed ourselves."

"They'll carry me at the co-op until I sell my first crop."

"The smell?"

"This is a big farm. The wind will blow it away."

Amanda nudged one of the pamphlets. "We don't have pens like these." The pictures showed cement buildings, sloped floors, steel birthing stanchions.

"I've read how to do it without all that expense."

She felt his determination. "I won't help feed them."

"You'll see. It'll be worth it," Carl said. He switched off the light but neither of them slept, each bewildered by the other's emotion. For Amanda the farm was scenery: laughing with the boys on a green bank while shadows of clouds moved across the valley or reading under the lilac tree. Carl felt a deeper, more sensuous stirring: wheat absorbing the power of the sun, growing heavy and golden, sows multiplying themselves into hundreds of small bodies, their mouths eating, transforming the raw stuff of the earth into life. Amanda found that on the farm even Carl's love-making had grown more vigorous. She thought that, Antaeus-like, he was drawing his power from simple contact with the earth, but she was only partly right. Specifically his passion involved partaking with the plants and animals around him in the mystical process of creation—a desire that kept him from leaving any field unplowed.

The next morning Carl taped a projection sheet to the refrigerator. "This line represents our profits."

"Sure."

"Have some faith." He tapped the paper, which had "$4,000" written across it. Amanda was pessimistic: the sheet reminded her of the gold coin Ahab nailed to the mast of the *Pequad*.

17

C. J. pointed to the pattern of lines. "Doggie," he said. "Daddy drew a dog."

"I couldn't have put it better myself," whispered Amanda.

The breeder showed them photos of him standing with his prize-winning hogs. "Best in the county," he said, grinning as Carl paid forty-five dollars each for two piglets.

"See, we can sell for fifteen dollars more than I counted on," said Carl. The breeder didn't tell them that the current high market would swing to a low one in the length of a sow's gestation. Every hog producer in North America had already put sows with boars, engendering millions of piglets, which would create a tremendous glut when they hit the market.

Carl tied the piglets inside a gunny sack in the trunk. "This is how we used to carry pigs all the time." In fact he had hauled pigs only once, in the back of a pickup.

Half an hour later Amanda found herself looking down at Carl, who had flung himself on the ground and clamped his mouth onto the muzzle of a limp piglet. The other one lay half out of the gunny sack, its breath rasping.

"Good Lord, Carl," Amanda said.

"She cost . . . forty-five . . . dollars," said Carl between breaths. "And I'm not going to let her go without a fight." But the piglet's triangular mouth was too wide. Instead of pushing air into its chest, Carl blew bubbles of froth out the corners of its jaws. "Think, Carl," he shouted. "Think." Suddenly he snapped the mouth shut and blew through the nostrils. The small chest bellowed out.

"You're too late, Carl," said Amanda.

"Damn," he said, flinging the body away. "At least I'll know what to do next time." Carl inspected the car and found a layer of plastic on the back of the rear seat, installed by the manufacturer to keep dust from going in and out of the trunk.

After burying the dead piglet in the alfalfa field, Carl put the other, which Amanda named Leah, alone in the pen. She sniffed her water, trotted around, and nuzzled the grain in her trough.

"Eat hearty," said Carl. "You have to grow as big as two sows." C. J. climbed in to pet Leah. Amanda, holding Sammy, laughed with Carl as their son waddled after the darting piglet.

"Mother, Carl is not stupid," Amanda said on the phone. "He just doesn't know hogs."

"You mean, he doesn't know his own limits."

"That's why I love him. He's not afraid to try anything."

"Tell him to try studying. Tell him to forget about pigs."

"He thinks he can make a little money," Amanda said.

"Do you need some more help?"

"No," lied Amanda. "We're all right now."

"What's his dissertation going to be—*Cognition in Hogs?*" Her mother was laughing.

Carl bought feed from the co-op at eight dollars a hundred, and Amanda looked from the five bags to the garden which was just sprouting. "More oatmeal and turkey legs," she said.

"Soon we'll have ham and chops and corn and tomatoes."

"By next week?" she said, walking back to the house.

By August Leah was large enough to breed. Carl rushed home each night from school to examine her bud-like vulva. The pamphlets said that when she was in heat, her organ would become inflamed. Carl inspected closely, but not having the sensitivity of a boar, he couldn't perceive any change.

"Come and look," he said to Amanda. "Maybe you can tell."

"I'll be damned if I will," she said. His feelings hurt, he returned to following Leah around her pen. Finally one day he saw. Her vulva had swelled to twice its normal size and turned red. Leah was nervous, trotting on dainty hooves, two hundred and fifty pounds of sow in heat. Their neighbor five miles away would loan his boar.

"Hurry," Carl said, gleefully. "We've got to get her while she's hot."

"We?" replied Amanda sarcastically. She loaded the boys into the car and remembered what her mother said about men and prolonged adolescence.

Carl drove quickly, his light trailer swaying back and forth.

The boar weighed six hundred pounds and wouldn't budge from his feed trough. The farmer beat the hog's side with a board. "Yo, Zeus," he said. "It's time to meet your sweetheart." Zeus lifted his head and squealed in a high pitch.

"Are you sure he can do the job?" said Amanda.

"You just get him with your sow," said the neighbor. "He'll perform like he's possessed." He shoved a bucket over the boar's head. "There's only one way to drive a hog." The boar backed quickly, trying to free himself, and the farmer steered him up the ramp into the trailer. Zeus shook the bucket loose, but before he could charge out, Carl had fastened the rear gate.

The boar's weight flattened the springs into a straight line, so the trailer banged against its axle as Carl drove home. He watched through the rear view mirror as Zeus lifted the gate out of its slot. Carl slammed on the brakes, and the boar crashed against the front of the trailer. "If I stop, he'll jump out. We'd never get him in again."

"Don't stop," said Amanda. She wasn't happy about the prospect of Carl backing a boar four miles down the highway.

Carl drove in jerks, jamming on the brakes whenever the boar tried to move toward the open gate. Each time Zeus was thrown to the floor with a blow that made the car shudder. The two boys started to wail; the boar shrieked; and the gate clattered as it dragged across the blacktop, hanging on by one strand of bailing wire. Amanda shut her eyes and held her boys.

When they reached home, and Carl backed up to Leah's pen, Zeus was too weary to stand. "He may have heat prostration," Carl said. Finally the boar roused himself and lumbered out. He upset Leah's water trough and flopped in the puddle. While Leah pranced nervously in and out of her shed, the boar lay in his wallow, panting, unable to move.

Carl made the boys watch. "I want them to learn how natural everything is." They all stood in a line, observing the panting boar.

"Get up," said Carl, poking him with a sharp stick. The boar grunted but didn't budge.

"Lazy pig," said C. J.

"Maybe they don't like us staring," said Amanda.

"Don't be silly," said Carl. He sent her and the boys away anyway and peered at the boar from behind the shed. "Come on," he whispered, anxious for something to happen before Leah's time was past. The boar rose at evening and ate all of Leah's feed before collapsing again. Carl sprayed him with the hose, trying to lower his body temperature, but he only grunted contentedly. Early the next morning when Carl sprayed him again, Zeus rose, shouldered Leah into a corner, and after two grunting tries finally chinned his massive weight high enough to service her. "Amanda!" shouted Carl. "You're missing it!" But Amanda was still asleep.

During the months of Leah's gestation, Carl built a triangular farrowing house with boards nailed at angles along the sides. When Leah rolled her bulk back and forth, the piglets would crowd under the boards and escape being crushed.

Winter came before Leah's projected delivery time. Carl went out each evening, and while she was eating, he tried to milk the rows of nipples covering her belly. After milk showed she would farrow within a few hours. But she wouldn't stand while Carl reached under her, and her teats were broad, like those of a woman, so he couldn't grasp them between forefinger and thumb as he had milking the cow on his grandfather's farm.

Amanda grew tired of Carl rushing into the barnyard when he came home from school. "We never talk anymore," she said. "You're seeing someone else, aren't you?"

Carl smiled and dragged her out with him. "Look how large Leah is. I bet we get twelve her first farrowing." Carl stood behind Amanda, his arms around her, watching Leah's maternal belly as dusk gathered. "We should get pregnant too," he whispered. Amanda looked over her shoulder into his intense eyes.

"One breeding at a time," she said, pulling away and walking back to the house.

Finally one evening a drop of white liquid beaded on a nipple. Carl shuffled repeatedly through the snow to flash his light across Leah.

"Go to sleep," Amanda said. "Just let nature take its course."

Carl was worried about the snow and the falling temperature. "I've got to be there when she farrows." Nothing happened. The next day he was so tired he couldn't drive to school. Deciding to sleep that night, he set his alarm to ring every hour.

Leah delivered herself at 3:15, and by the time Carl got to her two of the nine piglets had fallen out into the snow and died. Using an axe he chopped a hole in the frozen alfalfa field and buried them under chips of soil. In the morning he took Amanda and the boys out to see the living piglets.

"Tiny mammals," Amanda said. Pink and fuzzy, they were similar to large baby mice except for their gelatinous hooves.

"Look at them, Amanda, look at them." He passed one through the fence to each of the boys. Carl Jr. was careful, but Sammy dug his fingers into his piglet's belly. It squealed and Leah charged out. Carl turned, seeing nothing but her mouth, her jagged yellow fangs, and leaped backward over the five-foot fence. Amanda quickly passed the other piglets back to their mother.

"That's odd," Carl said. "She's never done that before."

Amanda shouted. "Don't you *ever* go in that pen again!"

"Don't worry. I don't have a death wish, you know." The two boys were crying. Carl walked them toward the house to keep his legs from shaking.

When the piglets were three weeks old, Carl decided it was time to castrate the four males. Eunuch pigs, he had read, grew softer, more ample flesh. After watching a video at the county agent's office, Carl gathered his knife and a bottle of diluted iodine and sat on a bale of hay, trying to figure how to get the patients out of the pen. He filled Leah's trough and then scattered some feed on the ground in the opposite end of the pen. After the piglets congregated, nuzzling the scattered grain, he climbed in and grabbed two by the hind legs and flung himself over the fence as Leah came screaming, her jaws unhinged.

He put one in a box and tied the legs of the other with twine, but it squirmed free when Carl started the incision. "Amanda," he shouted. She walked slowly out. "I can hold its body between my legs if you hold its mouth and forelegs."

"No," she said. "I still have *some* self-respect."

"I've caught these two. What am I supposed to do? I don't have time to get someone else to help me." Amanda reluctantly held the pig while Carl cut, opening the fatty tissue to find the gonads. The piglet twisted itself and squealed louder than seemed possible. Amanda jerked her hands away. The piglet twisted free from Carl, who lunged and grabbed it again. "Hold him this time," he shouted angrily. Amanda bore down, one hand clamped on the small animal's mouth, the other on its rib cage. Leah flung her forefeet over the top of the fence, shaking her froth-filled mouth and screeching like a harpy. After both piglets were castrated, Amanda slid them into one side of the pen while Carl reached over the opposite fence to grab another male. Leah snorted at the piglets, smelling the blood on them. While doctoring the next one, Carl looked up and saw C. J. and Sammy ten feet away, observing. He nodded toward the two boys.

Amanda nearly dropped the piglet. "Get in the house this instant," she shouted. The two boys ran into the fenced yard, where they peered through the slats of the gate.

"Just one more to go," Carl said.

Amanda's eyes were fixed on the boys. "How can they be normal after watching their father castrate helpless babies?"

Leah charged toward Carl whenever he approached the fence. Finally he scooped the last one up with a net of chicken wire he had tied onto the end of a two-by-four. They were finished.

"Don't ever, ever ask me to do that again." Amanda marched toward the faucet to wash the blood off her forearms.

That evening C. J. scraped his forearm on a nail: a line of blood beaded. Carl washed the cut and reached for the bottle of iodine, but C. J. jerked away. "No," he said, shaking his head and backing away from his father. "No, Daddy, no." Carl put his face into his hands, laughing.

"What else can he think?" said Amanda, trying to comfort her son.

All seven piglets grew rapidly, and soon Carl sold the males for $20 each, less than half of what he paid for Leah. Not wanting to borrow his neighbor's ancient sire again, he bought a half-grown boar.

During the next summer, before the three females were large enough to breed, Leah produced another litter, fathered by the young and energetic boar. Leah was passive during labor, and Carl helped her, moving across her wide, convulsing flank to lift the afterbirth away and to dry the piglets with a piece of terry cloth. The last one, a runt, was trapped in the afterbirth and suffocated before Carl could free it. He sold all of that batch as weaners, realizing that with his dilapidated sheds, he couldn't deal with more than four producing sows at once.

The triangular shed was for birthing, the other pens would be nurseries. "Dr. Carl," he started calling himself, his iodine wrapped in a square of burlap, ready for their umbilical cords.

The first farrowing went smoothly; however, that night two piglets were crushed by their mother's movement. Carl buried them in the field. Because of the summer heat, the sow moved her litter out of the protective house. She lay on two more that night, one the next, another the next. When Carl came home from school each afternoon, he lifted the blunt-snouted animals in his shovel and dug holes for them. He couldn't persuade the sow to move back into her house. Worried that she would trap her young against the wall of the shed, he nailed boards along its length. Despite his effort, that night she lay on another, leaving only three in her litter, including one cripple.

"How can a mother be so stupid?" he asked Amanda. "Lying on her own young." Amanda played with the boys in the yard, keeping them away from the sheds.

Despite his careful calculations two sows farrowed on the same day. Carl saved five piglets from the sow in the triangular house, but Leah farrowed in another pen, smashing four of her ten the first night. The next day Carl found three more tissue-thin bodies and the remains of a fourth, partially eaten. Though he removed them quickly, hoping Leah wouldn't get a taste for blood, the next evening he found another one dead, a head with no body. He lay motionless, thinking about the white, hulking sows who ate their young and about the livid patch of green which grew thick and beautiful over the skulls. Amanda touched his face, his chest, but he refused to be consoled. "We don't need the money that much," she said.

For Carl it wasn't the money. He had put boards all around every pen; he shoveled dirt and hay away because the soft matter could trap the piglets. "I can't stop the dying," he said.

"Take them away from their mothers."

"They'd starve without milk."

The next day Amanda went out with a two-by-four, trying with the leverage of the board to keep the sow with the largest brood off her piglets. The sow became excited and stepped on the leg of one, crippling it. Amanda flung the board against the wall of the shed and stomped back to the house.

Carl didn't bother to put the last sow in the farrowing house. She too lay on most of her piglets. Even when Leah's young were almost two weeks old, he found another partially eaten skull. He climbed slowly into her pen with his shovel, his back to the sow, to scoop up the remains. He heard Leah's scream of rage as she knocked him down from behind. He twisted underneath her, feeling her jaws working on the back of his leg. Shrieking he jammed the blade of the shovel into her yellow eye, into the pit of her mouth. He kicked himself backward on the ground and thrust the shovel again and again at her, until he felt Amanda pulling him up the fence from behind. He thrashed his arms and legs, forcing himself up and over. Leah roared open-mouthed; her two remaining piglets cowered in the far corner.

When Carl came back from the hospital with fifty stitches in his leg, Amanda had already sold the pigs. She gave the money to the feed store, but a bill remained of over five hundred dollars.

"You're creative," said Amanda's mother to Carl. "You'll find another project to prolong your education."

Amanda held him tight in bed. "Raising pigs is worse than gambling," she said. "Next time you get an urge, we'll take the money, drive to Wendover and enjoy throwing it away."

"Right," said Carl, thinking he should wait for another opportunity. He swung his hand down to touch the pamphlets on beef cattle which he had slipped under the bed.

••••THE ■
inter −
VIEW

Tom looked at the sweat shining in the palms of his hands. Wiping them on his slacks, he opened the door into the stake president's office. A man behind a desk placed a paper onto a stack, stretched his chin upward, unbuttoned his top button, and pulled his shirt open at the collar. He glanced at Tom over his glasses. "You here to see President Williams?"

"Temple recommend," said Tom. He touched his pocket.

The man nodded toward the door marked "High Council." "They're still going strong." He stood and leaned across his desk, his hand extended. "I'm Brother Clark."

Tom shook Brother Clark's hand. "Tom Mathews," he said and sat in a chair against the wall.

Brother Clark glanced at the clock. "Shouldn't be much longer." He leaned back in his chair. "Actually, they've been improving. Their meetings only go over a half-hour now." He lifted another paper from the stack on his left. "They've got too much work to do."

Tom rubbed the place above his right temple where the hair was thinning. Then he stood and walked to the bulletin board. There was a calendar with a picture of the Provo Temple at night. Next to it was a pink Happiness-Is-Family-Home-Evening sign.

"You're getting married, right?"

"Yes," said Tom. "How'd you guess?"

"I was here when President Williams got your call." He wrote something on a paper. "When's the happy day?"

"The first of next month." Tom walked back to his chair and sat down again, pulling at his pant legs where his garments were creeping up.

Brother Clark took off his glasses and stretched back, his hands behind his head. "He said something about this being the one he'd been waiting for. He likes to see good marriages happen. Used to be your bishop, didn't he?"

"Before my mission." Tom put his hand to his front shirt pocket and took out his recommend. "I was his priests' quorum assistant once." He looked at his new bishop's signature. Underneath was the blank for the stake president's.

"They don't make them much better than him." Brother Clark pointed a thumb toward the meeting room.

Tom nodded, frowning. "Dad said he's aged quite a bit."

"Especially since he's been stake president," Brother Clark said. "I've watched a lot of people come in here. They talk to him; then they leave and go on with their lives. They don't see him drag himself home after a night of interviews." Brother Clark stood to reach more papers from a file cabinet. "The worst on him are the young people. I mean the ones just back from their missions. They come in looking like they've just walked out of a seminary filmstrip, but later I read in the paper, 'Marriage to be performed in the home of the parents of the bride.' I wish they could see how he looks after they leave."

Tom rose and walked to the door leading out. "I'm a little thirsty," he said, feeling Brother Clark's eyes on his back as he shut the door behind him. Out in the hall he bent over the fountain, then turned to look into his former ward's trophy case. The dustier awards had his and his friends' names engraved on them. "100% Attendance – 1964." Bishop Williams had given Tom and another priest that one. "Aspen Valley Woodlore Contest – 1st Place." "Stake Basketball Champions." These too had been won under Bishop Williams's direction. Next to the trophies was a colored map of the world with pins stuck where missionaries were. None were in France, his old mission. He tried to find Fontainbleau but it wasn't on the map.

He walked down the hall to the priests' old classroom. The sun had shone through the east window, pleasantly warm on Sunday mornings. Bishop Williams had planned camping trips with the quorum in this room and told stories from his mission. Tom had anticipated his own.

Bishop Williams taught them about the gospel, waving his arms and laughing, scrawling words and pictures across the blackboard, making his quorum stand and repeat memorized verses. "The first principles and ordinances of the gospel are: first, Faith in the Lord Jesus Christ; second, Repentance . . . "

Tom turned back toward the office, pushed into the rest room, and washed and dried his hands. He watched himself in the mirror, then flicked off the light. The fan died with a rattle.

He looked out through the front door at his car; he could leave now and avoid facing his old friend. Standing by the water fountain, he touched his stomach where it was tight and took a deep breath. Then he shook his head and turned back to the office.

He waited at the door, listening. Finally he heard voices inside and went in. George Peterson, a high councilman, turned when the door opened. "Tom!" He reached for the younger man's hand, drawing him close with his other hand on Tom's back. "It's been awhile; we were happy to hear the good news." Tom nodded and returned the handshake quickly. He turned away to look through the door into the high council room, seeing the stake president still

29

talking to several brethren, smiling and gesturing. He had always reminded Tom of John Wayne, that is until he spoke; Bob Williams's voice was much deeper and he didn't have a drawl. Tom looked at the lines in his face, at the shoulders sloping more than Tom remembered. President Williams looked out through the doorway and beckoned Tom in.

"This is Tom Mathews, one of the best ever to come up through the Aaronic Priesthood. Tom, this is Brother Gilger, Brother Christensen, . . . ," President Williams said, nodding to the other men. "Tom's decided to settle down and start a family." He beamed at the others. Tom smiled briefly, then moved back, waiting until the president was finished. They walked together past the clerk into the president's office.

The older man closed the door and they stood facing each other. He put his large hands on Tom's shoulders. "You're looking good. It was a joy to hear your news." Tom hesitated, then laid both hands nervously on the president's arms.

"Well now," President Williams sat behind his desk, "let's have the whole story. How did you meet—" He looked at a piece of paper on his desk—"Carolyn?"

"At the institute at school."

"University of Denver?"

"Right. Carolyn and I were in the same class, and the teacher asked us to be on this committee together."

"Oh, a little match-making, eh?" Tom didn't smile. The president looked at him. "Well, you know this can't be final until I pass judgment. That's what we agreed, wasn't it?" He smiled across at Tom.

The young man nodded, holding his hands tight against his knees. He looked straight at President Williams, silently. The smile faded from the older man's face. He leaned forward, lifted a pen from his desk, and turned it in his fingers.

"We kind of lost touch with you in Denver."

Tom nodded.

"You worked for your dad's old partner out there, didn't you? Ah . . . what was his name?"

"Monte Daniels."

"Oh, yes. Lived in our stake awhile." The president leaned back, talking easier now. "Cement contractor, isn't he?"

"I tied iron for him."

"Then when you came back you met your fiancé?"

"Yes."

The president folded his hands across his middle. There was silence. He stuck his finger into his collar and pulled on it, then he leaned forward again. "Something's wrong about the wedding?"

"Yes."

The clock whirred.

"You want to talk?"

"Yes."

Silence. The president rubbed his forehead. "You have cold feet, Tom?"

"No."

President Williams turned his chair to one side. "Did you get involved?"

Tom was quiet.

"You know you can be forgiven for that if you have." The president turned suddenly to Tom. "Did you get sexually involved?"

Tom shook his head. "No."

Brother Clark's chair squeaked in the outer room.

"I don't think I can do it." Tom looked at his hands.

"Get married?"

"Yes." Tom looked up. "You asked me if I'd slept with Carolyn. I wish I had."

"What? What did you say?"

"I wish I had. If I'd done that, I could repent. And then go on. It'd be over then. But I can't repent of what I am."

"What you are? I don't—" The older man pushed his hand along the side of his face and up through his hair. "Maybe if you'll just tell me exactly what's happened." He put his hands together on the desk.

"It started on my mission," said Tom.

"What did?"

Tom opened his mouth then shut it.

"Something happened on your mission?"

Tom let his breath go out. "I had a junior companion once who wasn't–ah–. He didn't get up on time, didn't study, didn't like to go out. Homesick." Tom looked up at President Williams and back at the corner of the desk. "I talked him out of going home every week for a month. Every night I prayed that he would stay. I don't even know why I did it." Tom felt his face and ears grow hot. "We fasted one Sunday. After church we went up on this hill outside of town. I prayed, then he prayed. He stayed on his knees a long time and then started telling me how he was going to work harder and a lot of things like that." Tom looked up. "It made me feel glad," he said, his voice thick.

"I imagine it would," said President Williams, frowning.

"That night after prayer, I lay in bed. I just kept looking at him. When I thought he was asleep, I got out of bed and prayed again. Then I went over and stood by his bed and–" Tom looked at his hands.

"Go on."

"It was creepy. I got this idea of blessing him. Of putting my hands on him and blessing him. So I knelt down and I did." Tom's voice was shaking but he didn't take his eyes off the president.

President Williams spoke slowly. "You loved your companion and had been through quite an experience with him. Don't misinterpret what happened. I don't see–"

"What was wrong was how I felt. I was warm all over, and I couldn't move my hands. I just kept–"

"Touching him," the president finally said.

32   "Yes. I touched him."

"Where did you touch him?" the president asked, looking out the window.

"On the chest." Tom put both hands on his own chest.

"He didn't wake up?"

"I almost hoped he would, but that night I thought he was asleep. I found out the next day I was wrong. Even now I can't understand why he lay there awake and didn't move away from me. Anyway the next day while he was studying, I walked up behind him and put my hands on his shoulders. He jumped up and shouted, 'Don't ever do that again!' That week I was transferred to the mission home."

"Are you sure you were transferred because of what happened?"

"I think so. When I first got there, the mission president gave me a long interview. No questions. Just talked. About how nice it was to come home at night to a wife and children. He told me about the pleasure of seeing his wife pregnant with their first child. 'It was the greatest thrill of my life,' he said."

President Williams rubbed his eyes.

"At the end he was really serious. He said that some elders get weird ideas and are sent home early. He said that it's a waste because if they'd just control themselves until the end of their missions, even if they did have powerful tendencies, then they could marry a good woman and that would settle them."

"Maybe he was jumping to a conclusion about you."

"No, he wasn't," Tom said quickly.

"Maybe you're jumping to a conclusion about yourself."

"No." Tom moved forward on his seat. "After I was in the mission home, I started thinking, fitting some things together."

"Like what?"

"Once before my mission, a bunch of us were riding around after M.I.A. We ended up parking on the hill outside of town. I was sitting next to Stacy Bingham, and I knew she wanted me to kiss her, so I did." Tom frowned. "It wasn't anything like I thought it would be."

33

"You didn't like it?"

"I pushed her away. She said she wanted to go home."

The president smiled, then stopped. Tom hurried on. "Another time was when I was much younger, you remember, when we lived next to Sweeny Hansen." Tom's face was red and he watched the president as he talked. "One day I was playing out back and Sweeny was working in his garden. He stopped to urinate and saw me watching through the fence. He came over laughing, didn't do his pants up. He said something. I can't remember now, but I can still see him standing there. I could never stop thinking about it."

President Williams looked at Tom a moment, then spoke slowly. "I don't want to minimize what you've said, but you've confessed to me, and a lot of young men are confused about themselves as they grow up. It passes."

"Bishop, I'm thirty years old."

They both waited. "Have there been other experiences then?" President Williams asked.

"Yes."

Tom was silent.

"Like what?" The president waited. "You need to tell me." He turned in his chair. "Does Carolyn know any of this?"

"No. I tried a few times but I never could figure out what to say."

"Do you think she could handle it?"

"I don't know."

"If you think you have a problem, why did you get engaged?"

Tom was silent.

"Tell me how it happened, Tom."

"I told you we were in the same class. So we started studying together." Tom looked up. "I liked to talk to her. It's really hard to talk to most people, but we could go on for hours about anything. I just enjoyed knowing her. But then she started doing things like taking my hand, holding my arm against her while we walked somewhere. I hated it." Tom swallowed. "But what could I do? I couldn't say, 'Please get your hand off me.' Once I just said we should break things off. Then every time I went into the institute, she was there. She didn't understand. It was like slapping her face every time I passed her and ignored her. So I stopped going to institute. But then my college bishop called me in. After that I went back. I saw her and we talked; we started doing our homework together again. She thought it meant something. Instead of being easy like before, it seemed like she expected something."

"It's called wanting to get married."

Tom didn't smile. "Later our institute teacher called me in. 'You know Carolyn loves you,' he told me. Then he started talking about all the missionaries who come home and wait for the perfect girl. They get too fussy and then they're thirty and not married. He thought I didn't want to marry her because of her looks." Tom hesitated. "It started me wondering. Maybe I was confused. Maybe if we went ahead and got married things would work out, so I proposed."

"Do you think she's pretty?"

Tom looked at the floor. "I guess so," he said. "But I feel only friendship for her. When she tries to get close, I feel uncomfortable."

"It begins with friendship." The president frowned.

"I know that, but don't you see?" A bead of sweat ran down Tom's face. "I enjoyed her as a friend and I like her as well as anyone I've met, but I can't marry her."

"Just because you're not sure you like girls?" The president gripped the side of his desk and then sat back down. "Tom, you're like a son to me, and I don't want to see you hurt. If she's the fine girl you seem to think she is, love could grow."

"Sexual love?" Tom asked. "Do you believe that would grow?" He slumped back in his chair. "I don't anymore."

"If all you've done is what you've told me, then—."

"Then it would be great." Tom stared at the wall.

"Something happened since your mission?"

Tom spoke slowly. "You remember how I was working for Dad right after my release?"

"Yes."

"Well, maybe three months after I came home, I got this letter from an elder who had been in my mission. He said he was living in Salt Lake and couldn't we get together and talk about old times. It surprised me. I hardly knew him. Later I figured out why he wanted to talk to me. By 'old times' he meant my experience with my junior companion."

The president shifted his recommend book.

"Anyway I'd go up to Salt Lake City every week for doors or lumber or something. Well, the next time I decided what the heck I'd stop in. At the very least we'd talk a little French and then I'd head back."

Tom watched the president as he talked. "His place was just northeast of Temple Square, near a park, in an old two-story house made into an apartment. When he answered the door, his shirt wasn't buttoned and I could tell he didn't have his garments on. Three other guys were sitting on chairs inside. They smiled and said hello, but he didn't invite me in to meet them. He said we should get something to eat. We went to a restaurant, and all the time he talked about the job he'd had teaching swimming in Los Angeles and about what was wrong with the church.

"He'd forgotten his wallet, so I paid for the food. Then he thought we should go to this place he knew for some music and dancing. It had been quite awhile since I'd gone out and had fun, so I went. The place was west of the temple, across from the train station. It was pretty crowded, though. Some girls were dancing, but mostly it was guys dancing with guys." Tom stopped and waited.

The president looked at his hands; then he looked up at Tom. "You stayed?" he said finally.

"Yes. I stopped in the doorway, but Rick—that was his name— he pulled me on inside." Tom was talking quickly now. "I wanted to get out of there at first, but I was curious, I guess. Rick, well, he moved around, talking and having a good time."

"How long did you stay?" The president's voice wavered.

"A couple of hours. Rick would touch my hand and then he'd lay his arm on my back. It seemed all right in that place for him to do that." Tom looked up. "I felt as if a burden had been lifted. As if I was finally able to figure something out. I could talk openly about my confusion without feeling stupid or guilty or wrong, and he related. It was like being in France and then suddenly you see an American, someone who speaks the same language. Rick knew what I was feeling before I felt it. That was more important to me than agreeing with him morally."

Tom could see President Williams trying to control his frown. Something burned in Tom's stomach.

"I went to see him every week for a while when I went in for Dad. Then I started getting uneasy about the whole deal. He was always trying to get me to come and stay with them. He said they needed another roommate to help with expenses. I felt bad for them, but I left anyway." Tom stopped.

"Why did you leave?"

"One day we went over to the community center to play tennis. When we finished, one of the guys got hold of my garments while I was showering and started waving them like a flag. I grabbed my things and left. I realized that I couldn't mix with people like that."

"You've never told any of this to Carolyn?"

"Not to anyone."

"Think again about how she'd take it if you told her."

"It won't work, President." Tom slid forward on his seat. "Oh, I think she'd forgive me. Or she might think that she could reform me. Maybe she could, but I can't handle the thought of pressure that way. One time this girl came to Rick's apartment. She said that she knew she could change me if I'd just give her the chance."

President Williams rubbed a hand down across his face. He held his fist closed on the top of his desk.

37

"Carolyn just wouldn't get it," said Tom. "It was hard for me not to go back to Salt Lake. I had to keep away from other places too. I'd see men and I'd want to talk to them because I knew why they were there. I'd look at them and they'd look at me. How could she stand to be with me? Can you imagine what life would be like for her, married to me?"

"Have you ever gone for professional help?"

"In Denver. I was making a lot of money and I saw all kinds of counselors. Two years. Some told me it was because Mom and Dad had only one child. Some said my mother was too dominant in our house. Then there were those who said it was perfectly natural." Tom felt sweat dripping down his back. The president had put one hand to his forehead and was leaning forward, elbow down against his desk.

"I knew I could never be happy that way, but then I'd walk to the bus station or through the park and watch the people there. I didn't do anything though. I just talked and felt lonely. One doctor gave me electrical shocks while I looked at pictures. Another gave me drugs to make me vomit when I got excited."

The president cleared his throat again. "We have some professionals in the church who have developed certain methods based on the gospel."

Tom started to say something, then he stopped and said quietly, "I don't think they'd do any good." He thought. "Do you?" he asked.

The president was silent. "Ah, sometimes they help," he said, looking down at his hands. "They aren't always successful."

"I don't think it's a matter of being cured. I've been this way as long as I can remember. If I was to be cured now, it would have to be something like a lobotomy. I wouldn't be me anymore." Tom realized he was talking too loudly and he softened his voice. "I think what I need to do is to learn to accept who I am and to live with it. I can learn to control it so that I don't bother anyone."

"Do you think you can hold your breath for the rest of your life?"

Tom waited until he could talk calmly. "That sounds like what Rick said: 'You're going to sit in church and sublimate? No one there can understand. If they ever get a hint of who you are, they'll shut you out.'"

The president cleared his throat. Then he reached over and closed his recommend book.

"I thought I had a chance with Carolyn, until just being friends wasn't enough for her." Tom sat back and started again, trying to keep his voice level. "I've tried to break it off, but I couldn't pass her without seeing pain in her face. What can I tell her? How do I describe myself to her? I like her. I've never talked with anyone like her. But I still look twice when I see some men walking on the street." Tom felt his body tighten again.

"Have you made any contacts since you came back?"

"No! And I never will."

"You've given up on just going through with the marriage?"

"I can't. When I was seeing Rick, we went to a sauna. It was a cover for men who wanted to get together. Rick went there to work out and make contacts. I was approached a couple of times. Once when we were leaving, two or three blocks from the place, we saw this guy getting out of his car. He was in the sauna every week, really friendly. When he was about twenty yards from his car, he saw us. I raised my hand to him, but he ducked his head and hurried past us. Then he went scurrying down the street looking both ways to see if anyone saw me wave at him."

President Williams let his breath out.

"Then we passed his car. It was a station wagon with a briefcase in the front seat. There was a lady's hair brush and a baby bottle next to it. On the back bumper was a Happiness-Is-Family-Home-Evening sticker. Rick laughed, 'There's somebody who has his cake and eats it too,' he said." Tom sat looking at his hands. "I could never live like that. I couldn't be that kind of hypocrite. I've been taught not to be promiscuous. I've always believed in that."

The president nodded; they were quiet. Tom took out his temple recommend and pushed it across the desk to President Williams, who folded it. Tom sat looking at the floor. Then he rose and walked to the door, stopping with his hand on the doorknob.

"What will you tell her?" The president moved wearily to the window, his back to Tom. Tom could see that his shoulders were sloped even more than when Tom had come in. He felt angry.

"Just that we can't get married. We haven't sent any announcements yet, so we'll only have to tell our families."

"It's going to be hard on her."

"I know." Tom wiped his hand across his eyes.

"She'll want to know why. You can't break it off without giving her any reason at all." The president slumped into his chair.

Tom's throat and chest were tight; he felt a buzzing in his head. The president started to say something.

"Can't you see it scares me?" Tom said. "How can I be wrong my whole life? You know sometimes when I'm out at my parents' place and I get up in the morning, I forget and it feels great. I haven't read or heard anything that says I'd have a good chance of changing by getting married. Isn't that right?"

The president nodded. "Probably," he said.

"I've thought about it and I don't want to do that to her. After what I've told you, could you want me to get married?"

The president didn't move.

"I think of being with her . . . after we're married. I don't believe I could ever love her physically." Tom's cheeks were wet. "But I can't deny myself any kind of sexuality, can I?"

The president's face was white. Tom, looking at him, knew that he saw the depth of Tom's fear. The president was blinking his eyes quickly.

"You can't give up," the president whispered.

"What am I going to do? You said a minute ago I was like your son. So I am your son. A homosexual. Your son. When I touched Rick, I felt good about it. Sexually good. When Carolyn touches me that way, it feels wrong."

Tom sat down, his hands clenched. He felt his neck tighten again. Tears ran down his face. "I feel like an insect pinned to a card. I can't move. I've prayed and prayed and I feel 'You're going to be all right.' And that's good, but it doesn't tell me what to do."

The president looked straight at Tom.

"What *am* I supposed to do?" asked Tom. "I want someone to tell me."

The president didn't take his eyes from Tom.

"I can't do it."

The president waited. Tom walked to the window and leaned his face against the cool glass. Neither spoke.

"It's better with it out." Tom said finally. "I waited too long to talk to someone." His shoulders started shaking. Tom looked back at the president, saw him blinking quickly, his face twisting.

"What are you going to do?" President Williams asked.

Tom walked to the door. "I'll tell her. I'll just tell her all of it."

"What then?"

Tom shook his head. "I don't know. Maybe I'll be back." He started to open the door.

"Tom," President Williams said.

Tom looked back.

"Remember, you're still my son."

a court
OF LOVE

When I returned from my mission, the sky was cloudless over Utah. My future seemed as expansive as the wide and sunlit desert to the west of the flight path. Gliding northward, I felt like a ripened seed flung between earth and heaven. Soon I would find a woman to marry, becoming one flesh with her.

Through the small windows across the aisle rose the blue-green Wasatch mountains, unbelievable after the flatland of Houston. Town followed town underneath the jet in the rain shadow west of the mountains: Nephi, Santaquin, Payson, Spanish Fork, Springville, and Provo. Fifteen minutes before landing, I cupped my hands against the glass and saw Rockwood far to the west – cottonwoods and Lombardy poplars isolated by desert. "That's where I live," I said to the man next to me.

"How long were you away?" he said.

"Two years."

He was a businessman to whom I had given a Book of Mormon with the angel Moroni embossed on the cover. I was trying to end my mission the way I'd begun—with whole vision. He extended his hand to return the book. "Here," he said. "An interesting idea though—Jews fleeing Jerusalem and finding the promised land in America."

I put my palm up. "I want you to keep it." I was having trouble keeping my mind on my duty to him. As the plane circled the Salt Lake airport, a stewardess leaned across the seat opposite, reaching her arms over her head for a bag. My seat mate glanced toward her rear and then caught my eye.

"I know you," his look said. "I was you once." He lifted himself out of the seat, following the stewardess up the aisle.

I settled back, worried that seeing Belinda, I would focus on her sexuality and be overwhelmed by the frustration of my loss of her and be unable to meet her as a friend.

In the terminal I saw my mother first, Dad following behind. Seeing them, something relaxed inside; I had long anticipated the pleasure. Everyone had always said my father's face and build were similar to Henry Fonda's, but I was surprised at how much he'd aged. My mother was smaller, more compact, darker haired; I couldn't think of an actress who looked like her. They came toward me without speaking to each other, without looking, so many years married that even walking together came without thought of the other as a separate person.

"You've gained weight," Mom said, putting her arms around me.

"Looks fine to me," said Dad. His voice was gravelly and rich. The sound of it came back quickly. It seemed that there had been no two-year gap between this hearing and the last.

"I meant it as a compliment." Her voice held a hint of sharpness for my father. "You were so skinny, there wasn't much to get a hold of before." Her arms squeezed harder; her voice had warmed for me.

When she let me go, my father performed what he had apparently planned before—a personal ceremony. With a hand on each of my arms, he stared directly into my eyes for nearly a minute, making me uncomfortable. "Glad you're safe." He gripped my shoulders and pulled my cheek against his. An unusually private man, he had never before given his affection to me so directly. I looked over his shoulder at my mother, wondering. She shrugged her shoulders, as surprised as I was. As we moved to the baggage check, they seemed to avoid touching each other. I took one bag and Dad the other.

"Y'all follow me," he said. I looked at him and he grinned. "Just trying to make you feel at home."

In the car Dad was silent. There was a verbal and emotional stiffness between my parents I hadn't remembered. I wondered if it had always been there, and I had been too naive to perceive it before.

We drove southward past the point of the mountain where the state prison now lay, and I thought about my great-great-grandfather, who'd been imprisoned for having three wives. His son, John, had also been a polygamist, one wife before the Manifesto, one after, for which he had been excommunicated. We crossed the gravel bar left by Lake Bonneville and drove west across the desert, passing nothing for sixty miles but sagebrush, jackrabbits, and a few cedared bluffs, a distance the jet had crossed in a few minutes. My father talked about Vietnam and the students who had refused to go. "I'm in favor of doing your duty, but I can't sanction war either."

"They show the quality of their minds when they take to drugs and free love," said my mother.

I felt ignorant about the war because of my two-year famine from news. I didn't know where the troops were or which side was in possession of what cities. My only occupation had been to do the Lord's work on earth. Mission rules had insulated me from the carnal and worldly—television, movies, radios, newspapers, rock music, anything which could pollute my soul and keep it from being a clear receptacle of the Holy Ghost. As we drove through the

45

desert toward Rockwood, I thought with a new ambivalence about my town's isolation. My grandfather told me once that the people in Rockwood weren't affected by the Depression; they owned the land they lived on; they raised all they ate, self-sufficient. Time was a slow cycle from season to season, steady and languid.

The air was thin, the sky wide and blue, and the desert bluffs were tumbled about the flat, forms which appeared grotesque to those who didn't live in the desert. I smelled sagebrush and dust. Once we passed an antelope, which paced the car for several hundred yards, forty miles per hour, then veered off into a ravine. I hadn't realized how much I had missed the desert. I gloried in the peaks on the horizon: they made me able to see farther, intensifying the feeling of limitless space.

As we topped the ridge and drove down the tree-shaded lane toward home, the air turned cool and moist. "No difference here," I said as we passed the neighbors' houses.

"Did you think it would change in two years?" said Dad.

I pulled myself halfway out the window and sat on the door, my hands on top of the car, the wind blowing my hair. "Hey, I'm home," I shouted, drumming on the roof. Brother Williams, the stake president, looked up from loading seed into his grain drill, resting the sack on the hopper and waving his hat. Sister Sorenson, who had taught me in Sunday school and had become a good friend during that time, looked up from her hoeing to wave.

"Get back in here." Mom was pulling on my pant cuff. "Save your breath for your homecoming sermon."

Houston seemed eons away. The irritation and discouragement I'd felt there the last month fell away like dried scales from the surface of my mind. I exalted in being home and free.

We pulled up to the house, which looked more run-down than I remembered. The trim needed painting and some shingles were twisted out of place on the roof. Built by my great-great- grandfather, our house was a two-story adobe brick, the largest in town. "I'll have time to fix the house up now," I thought.

Time was an open space before me. I had nothing to do but what I wanted, which was to work next to Dad on the farm, enjoying home and town with no pressure from school or church. I could stretch myself with solid physical work while I looked slowly for a woman. I would make no more mistakes. Most of the women my age would be married now to the missionaries who came home last year or to the men who didn't go on missions. Like Belinda. I thought about her letter being a Dear John. There had been more to it than that. "I will always hold your memory dear." But.

"Well, how does it look?" said Mom.

"Sweet after where I've been living." Our apartment had been in a renovated motel, dingy and filled with roaches.

"Needs painting," said Dad. "I've been meaning to get to it, but it seems so many other things are more important." He avoided my eyes. I had never known him to put off work. We were quiet walking inside.

After I unloaded the pecans from west of Houston and the sea shells from Galveston, my gifts for them, I changed into the oldest pair of jeans and the oldest t-shirt I could find. "Why are you wearing those things?" Mom asked. "We're going straight to town on Monday to get you new clothing."

"Leave him alone," said Dad. "I know how he feels." His voice had a force which surprised me. I looked at the two of them, trying to figure the ways they had changed. "I'm glad you're home," Dad said. "I went through it twice before with your brothers, but with you it was different. I kept imagining you getting some parasite or dying from heat prostitution." He emphasized the last word.

"Prostration," said Mom.

"Right," said Dad, his voice crisp and loud. "I guess I've got work to do."

"You mean you guess you want to get away from here. Your son's been gone two years, and I'd think you would like to stay and talk to him."

"I'm not trying to start something today," he said. "I don't want to have fighting on this day."

"Then you're implying that it's me who wants to start something."

"Just calm down, Emily."

I touched Dad's arm as Mom left the room, frowning. He looked at me and shrugged. They had never argued with anger in my presence before. I wondered at the hidden cause of my mother's anger, because what had been said didn't warrant the emotion she had showed.

We sat at lunch where I felt Mom's eyes on me. "Am I so different?" I said.

"Not really."

"When's the crew coming?"

"Simon and Nancy will be here in the morning, Mike tomorrow evening. One night together in this house is about all anyone can handle."

"Oh, it's plenty big," I said. "When James Darren had all three wives in here there were twenty-five. We're fewer than that."

"Maybe that's what started the foundation sagging, all those women in one house," said Mom. "I can't imagine not having my own space."

"No wonder James spent all his time working outside," said Dad.

"He shipped his wives out of the house. Made them homestead for him." My father glared at her. Then her face changed. "Maybe the foundation started sinking when John Rockwood brought a woman here immorally. Maybe that's when it happened." She met my father's eyes, smiling when he looked away. "Charley called," she said lightly.

"What'd he say?" He was my best friend, hadn't gone on a mission, probably never would submit his wild nature to one.

"He wanted you to call him back."

"What's he been up to?"

"He works in Salt Lake since he came home. But he comes out weekends. He has a girl but they're not married."

"When'll he ever settle down?" I said.

My mother smiled. "Belinda lives here with her husband."

I concentrated on my food. "How's she doing?"

"She's sick as can be."

"What's wrong with her?" I half stood out of my chair.

"She's sick with child," said Dad. "One inside her belly and another one in her bed."

"Eliot, he can't be that bad," said Mom. "Though I do think he's a little overbearing." Mom looked down at the table.

"Well, I don't have time to sit around all day," Dad said. "Back to work for me."

After finishing my food, I went out into the barnyard. It looked like someone else's place, not my father's. He had always taken loving care of everything on the farm. The plow was leaning against the fence, its greaseless surface red with rust. Some boards were loose on the barn. The milk cow had sores on her udder. She had pushed against the fence around the hay stack so she and her calf could reach through and eat. They would soon smash it flat and ruin more hay.

I found a hammer, some staples, and some bailing wire and began weaving the wire across the hole. I imagined someday taking over the farm from Dad, working it until every field produced its best, every animal was fat. I thought that I could take it back to its prime, if he was winding down. One of the things I'd have to face, I knew, was my father's mortality. I looked across at Dad walking down the road, his shovel in his hand. He stopped at Sister Sorenson's, who had been widowed as a young woman some years before my mission. Since then she had rented her farm out and raised her three children by herself. Dad started digging in the ditch in front of her house, cleaning the weeds out of it. I knew it was important to help others, but I wished Dad had done his own work first.

Charley called back that night. He'd arranged dates to a dance in Hamblin, the next town south. "Becky has a cousin visiting," he said. "I thought about you as soon as I found out she was here." His voice was unsteady, apparently holding some kind of mirth.

"Thanks loads." I was anxious to see and talk to girls, to try to get Belinda out of my mind, but I wasn't sure about going to a crowded dance on a blind date with somebody's cousin on my first night home. I couldn't tell from his voice whether he was just happy reindoctrinating me into the world of women or whether he was chuckling because of what the cousin was like.

"Give me a few days," I said. "Tell them we can't make it. Just you come over and we'll talk."

"Becky's determined to go," he said. "We're getting married, you know."

"Congratulations."

"Yes, next spring, we'll do it." His voice was relaxed. "Hey, you know the best way to get in cold water is to just jump in. Wanda's a nice girl and she's *real* excited to meet you. Help me out for once."

"What's she like?" I said.

"I can really only judge what one girl looks like, and that's Becky."

"So you owe me one."

I wore my suit and tie, but Charley, who rang the doorbell, pushed me back inside with one hand on my chest before the dates in the car could see me. "I'm not going anywhere with you dressed like that. Don't you own a pair of levis?"

"Just ones with patches on the knees."

He smiled his old smile, a quick grimace which showed both rows of teeth. "Well, they'd be better than this outfit."

I took my jacket and tie off and changed to a plaid shirt, but I had to wear my suit pants. We walked out to the car together. I felt silly for being so nervous, as nervous as I had been approaching the first door of my mission. After knocking, my companion had turned to me and said, "You take this one." I had thought as fast as I could, but when the woman answered, I froze up. "You go to church?" I finally blurted out. "Hell, no," she said and glared at me, daring me to argue with her. I just backed away from the door. My companion didn't help, laughed at me all the way back to the apartment.

"Howard, this is Becky Summers," Charley pointed to the front seat. She was a pretty, blond girl, and she leaned quickly across the seat to shake my hand. "And this is her cousin, Wanda Johansen." Wanda was plainer but with a nice smile. I climbed in and looked at the back of Charley's head.

Becky looked over her shoulder at me and giggled. I knew they had planned this so they could enjoy my awkwardness.

"Country looks good this year," I said loudly.

"It's nice in Sanpete this year too," said Wanda. "That's where I come from."

"Not as pretty as Houston though. It's green there ten months a year."

"You boys are so lucky to be able to go on missions all over the world," said Wanda. When I moved my head, I could see Charley's smirk in the rear view mirror.

"Houston had a hurricane while I was there," I said. "We had our apartment demolished by a tornado." It wasn't even true. But I spent the rest of the ride describing the bizarre weather conditions in Houston, without giving anyone else a chance to speak. I finished as we drove into Hamblin. As I talked, I watched Wanda, trying to discover if she understood that she and I were the butt of a joke. Walking into the dance, I didn't know whether or not to take her hand, so I did nothing. Once inside we sat for awhile, no one speaking. The band was playing "The Fool on the Hill" and Charley and Becky got up to dance, wrapping themselves around each other. Becky held him tight, but her face wasn't happy.

"Do you want to shake a leg?" I said, feeling like the man in the song. I thought I'd never recover.

"Sure," Wanda said. On the floor I placed my hand in the middle of her back, held her other hand, which was already sweaty.

"You know something?" Wanda said.

"What?"

"I think my cousin is wild."

"Oh."

"I'm not that way at all." She moved closer and her breasts bumped against my chest. After all my wanting to talk to a girl, look at and touch her, it was strange how uncomfortable I felt. I couldn't relax enough so that her physical presence wasn't overwhelming. If I could have talked to her, I would have moved beyond that barrier.

"Have you got a girl?" she asked.

"No." I felt like wearing a sign that said, "No, no one else is interested in me," but that would cause more problems than it would solve. I had heard of girls who would sit next to a guy they thought might be a returned missionary, prime husband material, brushing against his thigh to see if he wore temple garments. I noticed other girls looking at me. Wanda watched me watching and moved closer.

On the way home Charley drove to a rise west of town, where he and I had gone to park with girls before my mission. My last visit to the spot had been with Belinda, and we had taken advantage of the isolation. Through the evening as Wanda moved closer and talked less, I forgot my earlier misgivings and enjoyed being with her. The four of us left the car and walked along the edge of the valley, looking over the town.

"One time I was walking not far from here enjoying nature and I discovered more than I was ready for," Charley said. "Married people."

"Well," said Becky. "What's wrong with that?"

"Nothing," said Charley. "It's just that they ah—how can I say this in front of a returned missionary—they had partially or possibly completely disrobed."

"So?" smiled Becky. "They were married; I think it's kind of romantic."

"Oh, I forgot to tell you they weren't married to each other." He looked at me, giving me the same sly smile as when he watched my discomfort in his rear view mirror. "And you'd be surprised if you knew who they were."

Despite our closeness before my mission, the gap between Charley and me was wide. While I had seen the unhappiness between immoral husbands or wives among the people we taught in Houston, I wasn't offended by the mere mentioning of sin. What saddened me was the way Charley, once my best friend, assuming it would shock me, tried to use it to shock me.

Wanda made incredulous noises.

"Scrud," I said.

"Scrud?" said Charley. "Is that a Texas word?" He laughed. "Scrud, you make me feel warm all over," he said to Becky, putting his arms around her. "Must be the spirit."

"Charley," said Becky, "leave it alone."

Wanda and I walked back toward the car.

I was only about a mile from home. The strain of stretching for things to say to Wanda had worn me out. "Thank you," I said to Wanda. "I had a good time, but I need to be alone now. I live right down there," I said, pointing. "Maybe I'll see you another time."

I started through the brush in the direction of home. Though Charley shouted after me, I didn't turn back. But neither did he follow and try to talk me out of leaving. I felt bad for Wanda; she wasn't to blame.

The lights of town lay eastward. The sky was moonless, making the stars even brighter. Trying to work away the unfinished frustration of the evening, I sniffed the air, scented by alfalfa blossoms in the nearby field, and listened to the toads and crickets sounding around me. The atmosphere was thin, not like the hothouse Houston had been. It was good walking through the darkness, good

53

to be alone again after so long. The only other time I'd been by myself for two years was during transfers. Traveling two by two might keep missionaries from sin, but it was a burden.

Suddenly I saw someone moving ahead of me through the brush. I crouched and saw that the person was going the other way—a woman, taller than Wanda. She looked back over her shoulder toward the spot where I was hiding. I stood. "Is everything all right?" I asked.

"Yes."

I walked forward.

"I was just out looking at the stars," the woman said quickly, and I recognized that she was Sister Sorenson. "I'm always astounded by them." She turned toward me, carrying a blanket which she wrapped around herself, despite the warmth of the evening. "Where are you coming from?"

She talked too fast, moving her hands nervously, and I supposed I had startled her. "I was at the creek with some friends," I said. "I wanted to be by myself, so I thought I'd take the short way home."

"I saw your lights." She unwrapped the blanket and, holding it under her arm, wiped her hands backward across her face. "Too hot with that around me." She grinned at me. "I thought you were teenagers parking."

Walking next to her, I sensed the aroma of her body, an envelope of warmth, as if she had been running. It struck me that I was alone with a woman for the first time since coming home. I moved slightly away: she was older than I and had been my Sunday school teacher. "Not the place for a returned missionary to be, eh?" I smiled, glad to be talking to her, one of my favorite people.

"Not really, probably be good for you. Leads to good things."

I looked at her. "Not you too."

"Me too?"

"All I hear since I've been home are innuendos about getting married."

A small smile showed on her lips. She opened her mouth to say something but shut it again. She looked away from me to the mountain at the north of Rockwood. "Do you know when I had my first baby, it seemed like everyone in town was pregnant, where before I didn't notice anyone. No one talks about getting married like returned missionaries do."

I looked at her. "I guess so."

"It's better than loneliness."

"Do you still miss him?"

She was silent. "I'd better get back in to the kids."

"Yeah, if you saw us pull in, you must have been out here more than an hour." I waved my finger at her. "And who's watching the kids?"

"They can take care of themselves." The bitterness in her voice surprised me. "Sorry. I just get tired of them sometimes. Anyway, Kerry is almost eight."

I said nothing.

"I'd better get back in." She touched my arm. "It's good to see you again."

"Same with me. Do you know you're the only person I've talked to since I came home who has made any sense."

"Counting your mother and father?"

"They're different. I can't really tell how."

She walked faster. "What am I doing? I've got to get my horde bathed. See you Sunday."

"Yeah, Sunday." I stuck my head inside the door to her house, a white wooden building, which had been built by John Rockwood for his second wife. "Hey," I said to the three kids. "Don't give your mother a bad time." They looked at me with their mouths open.

I closed the door behind me, looking in through the gauze of the curtain as she drew her children to her. "Sammy kept thinking he heard someone outside," said Kerry. "We kept thinking it was you or Brother Rockwood, but nobody came. Sammy was sure lonely until I told him a story." She guided them through a door out of my sight. I smiled, walking across the lane toward my own house. Before I left on my mission, I hadn't noticed the strange turns toward bitterness that Sister Sorenson had shown tonight. My mother and father seemed also to have changed radically. I satisfied myself that they merely thought of me as an adult now, treating me with more directness and honesty. I moved slowly across the lane into my own yard. Mom was in the kitchen.

"Oh, I didn't hear you drive up," she said. "Did you have fun?"

"Sure. Loads."

"What happened?" she asked.

"Charley and I are different now, that's all. Where's Dad?"

"Ward teaching.

"Who are his families?"

"Just Sister Sorenson." I wondered why I hadn't seen him. "And here he is now." Dad opened the front door.

"That was a long visit," said Mom with the sharpness I had discovered she only used with Dad.

Her voice stopped him. "Just an hour, Madame Judge," he said, watching her. "Those kids. They asked me to tell them two stories each. I only just dragged myself away."

I was tired after my long day, so I started up the stairs toward my bedroom, only half listening to what Dad was saying. "You taught just the kids?" I asked. A warning had started in my head, holding me.

"No. She was there too. We had a good visit. Hey, maybe they'll give me you for a companion. Then I won't have to go by myself. It's just too hard to drive into town to get someone so I can come back here to one family just across the street from us."

I listened to my father's loud cheerful voice and wondered why he was lying. Then I remembered my mother's bitter voice, the blanket Sister Sorenson had nervously carried, the angle of my father's body toward her as he had dug in her irrigation ditch, her hand which had reached to touch his arm, and the mysteries of the evening clicked together for me. It was an intuitive leap on little evidence. My only defense is that I was a newly returned mission-ary. In my heightened awareness of my own sensitivity, in my ex-aggerated trust in my body and mind as perceiving instruments, I made a careless leap. It was only chance that I happened to be right.

Saturday the rest of the family came to honor me at my home-coming. My two brothers and my sister Nancy and all their kids made nineteen people, counting the babies, around the table. "You're either going to have to stop having kids or we're going to have to get more leaves for the table," Dad said before the blessing. Despite the bustle of everyone around, I knew Dad was watching me be-cause of my quietness, aware that something had changed.

Nancy sat beside me with her baby in a high chair and her husband next. She had gotten married after I left on my mission, and now the two of them touched eyes over their new child as they took turns feeding him. My older brothers and their wives sat across, one married five years, the other seven. They didn't look at their wives; they interrupted each other when they talked. I wondered how I would act toward a future wife: would we be courteous? Ev-eryone talked at once—a babble of noise—and I held my hands across my ears.

"Children, quiet down please," Mom said.

My oldest brother, Simon, looked at me. "Don't worry, Howie. Your time will come."

"My time for what—deafness?"

He laughed. "I suppose you think your kids will act better." He took more ham.

"Do you expect us to believe that you didn't notice any long-haired Texans?" said Mike.

"He's got one waiting in a room in Salt Lake until he can break the news to us."

Mom knew I was embarrassed. Dad spread his arms out, and I was afraid he would tell them to leave me alone, calling the hounds to the scent. "I'm glad all of you could come," he said. "I love all of you." The words intensified my awareness of his hypocrisy—smiling over his family, the picture of a good church member, touching the hand of the woman he was cheating. I stood and left the table, pushing the back door open and moving through the trees in the orchard. Soon Dad came out and put his hand on my shoulder. I moved from under his hand. "What's bothering you, son?" He waited. "Too much, too fast?"

"Yeah, that's it."

"Everybody's changed while you were gone."

I looked out at the dark green trees around Sister Sorenson's house. "Right."

"That isn't it, is it?"

"No."

"What is it, Howard?"

"I saw Sister Sorenson last night."

"Did you have a chance to talk to her?"

"I mean I was talking to her while you were supposed to be ward teaching her. You lied to Mom and me."

Panic came into his eyes, but with visible effort he fought it down. "I don't see . . . ?"

Turning, I walked toward the house. Because no footsteps sounded, I knew he had remained under the trees, looking at my back. I moved through the kitchen and started up the stairs toward my room.

"Come finish your dinner," Mike said.

I walked up the stairs without turning.

"I thought you might sit and talk with us," Mom said.

"I'm still tired from the trip and everything." I shut my bedroom door behind me. I had shocked him, then left. Doing that made me feel better.

Soon he knocked and came in. I spoke quickly before he could begin an explanation. "I know you met her there."

"Did she tell you that?"

"I cut through the brush from the creek. I got mad at Charley and came home that way."

"How long were you there?"

"What do you mean?"

"Ah, did you—?"

I waited, watching his embarrassment. "I didn't see you with her." He relaxed some and the slight doubt faded away which I had allowed myself to keep.

He looked at the door. "What are you going to do?"

"I don't know."

"I love her."

"Love?" I had difficulty saying the word. "How did you let it happen?"

He motioned me quiet. "Don't ask that. I don't have an answer."

"Great."

"At least not one you would understand right now."

"What are you going to tell Mom?"

He was silent. "That is between me and her." He looked at me. "Leave it that way."

I said nothing.

"I'm glad you're taking this so well."

My thighs and arms were shaking. "How do you know how I'm taking it?"

"I don't." He stood in the doorway.

"Please go away," I said.

"Yes, but I'm going to get through this weekend. The kids are all here. Give me that much." He leaned against the doorway. "Lord, I'm tired," he said. Then he left. The image of his face with its deep, downward lines hung in my memory, making me shiver. I looked at the shut door, angry now at what he had asked of me. I wondered what Mom would do if she knew. She'd probably leave him, go to live with one of my brothers. I heard voices downstairs and tried to imagine what Dad was saying to them. "Howard's not feeling so well."

Sister Sorenson had taught Sunday school with vitality and force. I had thought that if anyone was converted, she was. I lay on

59

my bed, wondering how it had started. Passing in the street, working together on church projects, helping with her ditches which needed cleaning each spring because she had no husband to do it, visiting her every month for home teaching. She might have joined him one night for the midnight water turn. That made her calculating. He may have asked her to help him move a canvas dam at night, though he could have easily done it himself. I hated them both for what they were doing to Mom.

Trying to imagine the beginning of their affair, I thought about how my relationship with Belinda had started and more of my old feeling for her came back, an uncomfortable emotion, because she was married now.

While the rest of the kids in MIA painted the scenery for the church roadshow, Belinda and I had crept separately down the stairs into the furnace room. "This is our own Mutual Improvement Association," she said. I was filled with wonder at the pleasure of my arms around her. We kissed, holding ourselves tight against each other. She undid her bra and let me curl my hand around her breast, a sin which burned when I tried to pray it out of my soul before my mission. We listened for the door to open at the top of the stairs. The next time we went down, Brother Thomas surprised us, or nearly did, and we each had interviews with the bishop for kissing in the cellar. "You are lucky you didn't go farther," he said. "Some things are so sacred they can only be performed inside the bonds of marriage." We dated as seniors, under tight supervision from our parents, who had been warned by the bishop.

I hadn't believed that I would ever want to be with another girl. Evenings in the car, we kept a thin blanket between us. "Fornication is next to murder in seriousness," the bishop said, and that fear had somehow kept the blanket in place.

One day Belinda changed. "We need to grow up and start doing the things we know are right," she said. "You go on a mission and I'll marry you when you get back." Making up my mind had been a process of fighting down my desire for her and my fear that she would leave me. If she had waited another month before her spiritual revival, we would have married. Or if she had waited my full mission we could be preparing for marriage now. I thought about the way she had looked when she said goodbye at the airport. I wanted her at that moment, a desire which tightened around me, evoking an ambiguous passion, powerful and druglike, deeply repulsive. Thinking about her as if she were free made me aware that I was a descendant of my father and of John Rockwood. My father had touched Sister Sorenson the way I had touched Belinda when I was nineteen.

I tried to argue myself out of my Puritan stiffness and anger about what my father was doing, but I could only think about my mother. He had broken his obligation to her. Most people I met on my mission felt that sexual morality was relative, but I couldn't work myself to thinking that way, despite the fact that it would have made things easier. My emotions vacillated: the house and even the entire town seemed a prison, with confounding laws and cruelty lurking in corners, behind trees and walls. My responses had narrowed, my sensitivity holding me rigid and hopeless in the face of my father's destructive act. And my father was a good man. Human nature seemed bound to destructiveness.

I rose suddenly. Taking the box filled with family photographs, I lay my parent's pictures in a row across the floor according to their ages, from their wedding to now. I was always surprised by my mother in her wedding gown; she was thin-waisted, her hair a downward curve on each side of her face. I tried to imagine my father and mother as two young people loving each other, making love, but I couldn't. I could only envision her aging body as Dad must see it now. Sister Sorenson was thirty. I quickly shoved the pictures into the box. "You are weak," I said and had no more feeling for the person my father was.

Before long my sister Nancy came up, but I asked her to leave. "I'm sorry, I'd like to talk, but I'm worried about my speech tomorrow. I want to make it a good one." Then because I told her I

61

would, I reread the journal entries which described the people I had converted, reliving the joy I felt with them when they accepted the gospel.

Toward late afternoon I finished my talk and decided to act as if nothing had happened between my father and me. As he and I went out to check on the cattle, he pressed his lips onto Mom's cheek. She touched her hand to the spot and her eyes went sad. I was the only one who noticed, and I wondered if he had done it for me to see. Dad drove to the middle of the field and shut the truck off. He was nervous, taking me by the shoulders and looking full into my face. "When you do find a woman, love her. That's the best thing a man can do; the hardest thing a man can do." Tears stood in his eyes. We fed the rest of the cows without talking. That evening we all gathered to the living room. Everyone else played cards, but I didn't feel like it. I lay on the couch pretending to doze.

As we walked into church, I saw Belinda across the room. She was slightly fuller, but not in the belly: she looked more like a woman than she had before I left. Mom pointed to Belinda's husband sitting behind the pulpit. He was a stocky man, a little older than me. Watching Belinda, I remembered the pleasure of loving her. I didn't want to talk to her, but she raised her hand and crossed the room toward me.

"It's good to see you," she said, nervous, looking away from me toward her husband.

"Yes," I said. Her eyes seemed veiled, tired and sad, I imagined, but then they caught mine and held them. She smiled and I wanted to get away from her as all my old feeling rushed back. If I could have, I would have taken the next plane back to Houston, anyplace to get away. "Why didn't you wait?" I wanted to ask.

"Well, Howard!" I turned toward the cheerful voice behind me and saw Wanda. "Becky doesn't go to church so I came alone."

"I'll talk to you later," said Belinda, smiling with what I interpreted as wistfulness. Feeling nearly desperate, I watched her walking away.

"I'm sorry about the other night," I said to Wanda. "Charley was getting to me, but it was pretty rude of me to leave."

"It wasn't the best situation I've been in either. That Becky is a real pill."

I looked again for Belinda but saw instead my father moving through the people who stood waiting for the meeting to begin, laying his hands on their arms, joking, friendly with everyone, as he had always been. Mom moved a little behind. I couldn't see her face until she turned half toward me: it was animated, laughing at one of Dad's jokes. She leaned toward him, whispering something. Dad put his hand on her arm. I couldn't see Sister Sorenson and her children yet.

"Becky is so different from when she was younger." Wanda looked at me; I could tell she was uncomfortable. Brother Ault passed, smiling and shaking our hands. "It's good to have you home." I wanted to be alone on the top of Joseph's Peak, looking down on Rockwood where some other poor fool was trapped by his relationships to people. Sister Sorenson came in and took my hand in both of hers before I could think. "I hope things go well for you," she said. After she left, finding a seat behind and to the left of my parents, I still felt her touch on my hand. Several people turned and smiled at Wanda and me standing together.

"Look at them," said Wanda. "That's what I hate about small towns; they've already decided something about us." I looked at the ward members, some of whom were still glancing toward us.

"Well, I'll see you," I said. "I've got to go sit on the stand." I sat next to Belinda's husband, who shook my hand vigorously.

"Brian Sharp," he said. "I'm second counselor in the bishopric."

"Howard Rockwood," I said.

"Yes, I know."

Wanda sat on the first row. I looked toward the back of the room, away from the people, many of whom were smiling and trying to catch my eye. I would have to speak to them soon. I had missed marrying Belinda because she couldn't wait, as my father

63

couldn't wait. The bishop rose. "I'm pleased to welcome you to Elder Howard Rockwood's homecoming," he said.

The meeting started with everyone singing "Ye Elders of Israel." I kept my lips pressed together. Barney Thompson stood to say the invocation. During the prayer I watched Sister Sorenson from partly closed eyes, trying to imagine what she and my father thought about in church. The thing between them must be kept in a box somewhere that they only opened at night when they were together. They would both go crazy otherwise. Then came the sacrament song. "Again We Meet Around the Board." The deacons moved down the rows with the trays of broken bread, the room quiet except for a few fussing babies. I wanted to walk to where my father sat and stop him from taking the sacrament. A person ate damnation to himself when he took the sacrament unworthily. I wondered if I believed that. My mother's arm was threaded in Dad's. How would her face be when someone told her about him?

When I was fourteen, Mom said I couldn't go to a dance in the next town. I talked to her for an hour in her room, until she was flustered. She turned to the wall and said, "No. No. No. No. No."

"You're nothing but a thick-headed bitch," I shouted, running out of the house. Nearly an hour later when I passed her room, she was still sitting, staring at the same place on the wall.

The deacon stood in front of me, the tray of bread extended toward me. I automatically took a piece and passed the tray, feeling the crumbly bread between my fingertips. The deacon was still watching, so I put it in my mouth and swallowed. The yeasty taste drew the saliva sharply. With the taste on my tongue, I tried to think about my speech. Instead I looked at Belinda and remembered the grayness of her eyes. I watched Belinda closely, thinking about kissing her, nearly feeling the texture of her lips.

After the prayer for the water, before the tray of small cups could come to me, I left the stand, aware that everyone was watching, and went into the bathroom. Standing in front of the urinal, I thought about what my father had done. When I was finished, I waited in the doorway, just out of sight, until the sacrament was over and the bishop was talking again. It was almost time. I could stand and describe what I knew about my father's adultery, as people did in the early days of the church. Dad, having been a missionary and having received the Melchizedek priesthood, would be excommunicated for his sin. He would be ignored by most of the members of the ward, a trial for him, but my mother would be hurt the most. I couldn't think clearly about what was best, so I returned to my seat.

An excommunication court is a court of love, they said. It can make a person realize his sin, which is the first step toward repentance. Knowing and not saying makes a person a party to the wrongdoing. Still I didn't know of anyone who had told the bishop about someone else's unworthiness. Of course I wouldn't know if someone told in private; the bishop would have kept it confidential.

In 1930 my great-grandfather had been excommunicated from the church for taking his second wife, forty years after the prophet said it was now wrong. The woman was thirty years his junior. Members of the church still remembered what he had done, having developed a revulsion toward polygamy as strong as that toward incest. Kids who went to the cemetery for a thrill said they could still hear him moaning. He was warning others against his mistake, people said. Once I found in my father's bedroom the metal box where my great-grandfather's diary was kept. "August 15, 1934. It has been three years since anyone in Rockwood has talked to me." I knew that the date of death on his tombstone was 1934.

At the pulpit the bishop talked about his own mission, years before. Then he introduced me. I stood and moved to face the people. "In a Spanish-speaking part of Houston lives a widow woman and her children, five of them. It was my first area before I moved to teach only Anglos. We had passed the house many times on our bicycles; the kids were always dirty and running wild. We knew from talking to her neighbors that she saw men in the evening for money." I looked out at the audience. Not even the babies were making noise. Everyone was waiting to see how much detail I would go into about the woman's unholy life. When I heard Belinda's husband clear his throat behind me and murmur something to the bishop, I felt like going into specific detail. "So we didn't go there. One day we had passed her house and I had the strong and certain feeling we should go back. When we knocked, no one seemed to be home. The door was open a few inches so my companion pushed it farther to call inside. There was a goat there, but no human was home. My companion wanted to leave then. But I made him walk around the house to the back." I couldn't develop much interest in my own talk. I took a breath and went on. "They were all there under the shade of a blanket. With a damp rag she was bathing the forehead of one of her children who had a high fever. We told her who we were, and she didn't want to talk to us at first. 'Go away', she said. 'Can't you see I have a trouble today?' I told her about the power the priesthood has for healing the sick. Then she let us lay our hands on her child to bless him. When we passed again that evening, she was waiting in the street for us. 'My son is well,' she said." I looked over the audience, remembering the weeks of teaching Sister Montoya. Her eyes had grown brighter and more clear as she learned the truths of the gospel. "She began surprising us. When we came to teach, she would give us the gifts of her sacrifices. 'Last night I told the men to go away. They are no longer welcome here,' she said one night. 'Today I took my wine and poured it out in the garden. I smashed the bottle.' One day she said nothing but her house had been scrubbed, the children bathed." One by one she had packaged the sins of her life and laid them aside. Watching from the outside, I knew her steps were firm, steady, as she moved toward her own salvation. She had been a simple sure woman, believing everything we said. Gripping the podium, I let her clear spirit fill me and I spoke from that feeling. As soon as I sat down, the clarity left me.

66

After all the visitors had left our house, abandoning the tables which were covered with cookie fragments and empty paper cups, I lay on my bed and thought about Belinda. She and her husband had been to the reception. He was shorter and heavier than I, guiding Belinda though the people in our living room with his hand firm on her elbow. I didn't have a chance to talk to her alone, and I didn't want to talk to her with her husband.

In the darkness I thought about putting my hands on Belinda, as her husband had, of taking her clothes off. My hands moved across her breasts, fuller now because of her pregnancy. I imagined my hand moving down her body. Suddenly I moved out of my bed and prayed. "Lord, I give you this gift. I will no longer think about her." But the thoughts returned. I had discovered an immutable and terrible law, that the impulses to love and to harm are incomprehensibly tangled.

The next day I stayed in bed, pretending to sleep. Finally, late in the morning, I heard my mother's footsteps, light, walking up. She knocked and opened the door, smiling.

"Oh, you're awake," she said.

"Yes, I guess I woke up when you knocked."

"I just wondered if things were all right."

"I don't feel good."

"I'm sorry," she said. "Let me get the thermometer."

"I already took it. A hundred and one. I took an aspirin." I was surprised at the lie. From the window I could see that it was raining, hard. When I was young, running in the rain had made me feel clean.

I heard Dad come into the house, and I went down the stairs and out into the field. The water was cold on my head and shirtback. Soon he followed, walking along the lane toward me. I heard his footsteps and felt something, a coat, laid across my shoulders. "You're sick," he said. "Killing yourself won't help anything." I let him lead me back to the house, glad to have his arms around me.

I sit in a wooden rocking chair in the high-ceilinged living room. To my left my father reads the newspaper, glancing again and again from behind it out the window. I can see past him the white skirt of light from the streetlight in front of Sister Sorenson's house. My mother sits on the floor, packaging odd socks and baby shirts in manila envelopes to send to my brothers and sister. "They always forget something," she says.

I wrap my arms around myself, against my mother's sad and my father's nervous eyes. The only sound is the rocking of the chair, the hard sound of wood crossing wood. A beat up, a beat back, waiting.

A house OF ORDER

Three weeks had passed since Howard and Sylvia Rockwood last made love. Earlier, before the days of silence, they could have begun casually, prompted by any minor conversational motion, finally drawing close enough for physical discourse, but now it would take singular effort. That morning, riding the fence to make sure his cattle couldn't climb through and be lost in the higher reaches of the mountain, Howard looked down on the fields of Rockwood. Perched on the slope, he felt that if he wasn't careful the cultivated green which was his life would slide away into the desert and dissipate in the dry heat.

Soon afterward he discovered a transparent skin rolled against the base of a cedar post, like a tendril of mist hidden from the sun. He dismounted and curled it in his fingers—the second rattlesnake skin he had found in his life. It could become a gift to help them talk, a prompt or a gimmick. Cradling the brittle shell, he rode toward town, which was caught midway between the western Utah desert and the watered communities of the Wasatch Front. His great-great-grandfather had settled the area under a call from Brigham Young.

At home he placed the intricately ribbed snakeskin on the kitchen table. "Sylvia, come see what I brought you." He blew and the transparent skin rustled against the salt and pepper shakers. "Sylvia?" He dropped his saddle bag with what was left of lunch on the wood stove, dusty in the summertime, and looked at the pans hanging on the wall. Suddenly he felt close to another, familiar universe, and he was returning from school to the same kitchen, wrapped in the same sunlight, calling for his mother. The only difference was that the radio played "Hey, Jude" instead of "Love Me Tender."

He looked at the electric stove; Sylvia hadn't started cooking. "Surprise," he called. "I've brought a friend home for dinner." The kitchen window was the old kind, installed by James Darren or replaced by his son with glass that distorted the trees on the other side, compressing and stretching the branches, but he could see that Sylvia wasn't in the orchard. "OK, where are you reading today?"

The bathroom door opened and she walked down the hall toward him, a book dangling from her hand. Wearing one of his shirts—too big for her, hanging straight from her shoulders, flat across her chest—she looked like a little girl. She bent over the skin, pulling her black hair sideways out of her eyes.

"A snake," she said. She knelt on the floor with her chin on the edge of the table. "Did you see him with his fresh skin?"

Howard shook his head. "I'm lucky I didn't. Dad told me that they'll strike at anything if you disturb them while they're shedding." The cover of her book showed a heavy-breasted woman lying in the arms of a cowboy. "I almost smashed it bringing it to show you."

She caught him looking. "The real west. I've been expanding my mind."

"Romance," he said. "The opiate of the Mrs." She made a face.

Reading all day, especially when she read trash, made her dull-headed and disagreeable. The cowboy had wide, muscled shoulders.

"I found it in the garage: I think it was one of your father's." She gave him a slight smile and walked into the living room. His father had indulged in romance, had tried to live fictions. "I'm almost finished," Sylvia called. Sticking her head back through the doorway, she nodded toward the snakeskin. "Thanks."

She was gone. Since the morning after the last time they made love she had acted this way—cold and distant. Or she made wisecracks, like the one about his father's stash of westerns. Howard had offended her either during the love making or earlier in a way that the love making emphasized, but he wished she would talk about it. Riding the fence, he had tried to decide what bothered her: (a) he had moved too quickly that night, leaving her unsatisfied or in some other way trammeled; (b) she was bored since she quit her job; (c) she had a secret lover, an option he didn't take seriously but inserted to make sure he covered everything; and (d), the most obvious choice, she had finally decided that living in his parents' old house, on his father's old farm, wouldn't work and she was using her body to imply what she knew would hurt him if said directly.

Two years earlier his father had left his mother. When he later died in an auto accident in California, Sylvia and Howard had interrupted school at the University of Utah, a sacrifice for both of them, and Howard began gathering into his own hands the reins his father had dropped. Howard's mother moved to Salt Lake, near his sister, and he and Sylvia established themselves in the old house. They had committed to a two-year experiment, which was halfway completed. Sylvia had grown up in Charlottesville, where her father taught at the University of Virginia, and she had surprised Howard by agreeing easily to the long sabbatical from school and city. As he plowed, planted, and harvested his land, turned his cattle out to feed on the mountain, he had been less and less able to think of their stay as temporary.

He looked past the skin toward the empty stove and counter. "Hey, what do you say if I cook tonight?" he called. She had quit her job at the insurance agency two months before and since then had been winding down.

"Fine," she said.

"Thanks." He pulled two steaks from the freezer and laid them in a frying pan, sliced several potatoes and an onion in with the meat. After pouring a cup of water across the food, he covered the pan with its lid. He washed and walked back into the high-ceilinged living room, drying his hands. "Anything wrong?" he said, knowing the answer already. Confronting her directly had never worked.

She looked up. "No. Why do you ask?" She turned again to her reading.

"All last night you sat there staring out the window as if I was invisible."

"I'm sorry." She looked up at him. "You look tired."

"And today—." She was reading again. "You're not listening to me."

She looked up, wide-eyed, holding her face blank. He stood and left the room. In the bathroom he sat on the toilet lid, his feet up on the legged porcelain bathtub while he unlaced his boots. He stood and slowly shook them out into the toilet. "I *am* tired," he said out loud, looking into the mouth of his boot. It was hard work making the farm produce as well as it had when his father was thirty, getting it to look as it did in memory. He was also tired of Sylvia's devices. "What is talking to your shoes a sign of?" he called down the hall.

"Did you say something?"

He pushed open the swinging door into the living room.

"Acute schizophrenia," he said.

"Are you talking to yourselves again?" She wasn't looking up from her book. But she was listening. She was staring at the page listening.

"A cute schizophrenic." He smiled across the room. "Can you

read and think at the same time?" He wanted to confront her with what she was doing to him. But that would bring anger.

"Of course not." She wouldn't admit her readiness to talk.

Without moving he let the door swing shut, standing with his nose against one of its panels. "Who do you think you're fooling?" he whispered. In the bedroom he changed out of his work clothes, gradually failing, despite his efforts at humor, to control his anger. He knew the joking meant nothing, but he was too tired for deeper talking. They would both wait in tension until the mechanism of her mind shifted, like an uncertain clock; nothing he did could move her faster. "You know Howard, I've been thinking," she would finally say. Then they would pour it all out for two or three hours, slowly becoming correct again. He thought of the pleasure, toward the end of their talk, when after the pain of digging up and cataloging feelings, they'd talk in rhythm. After the communication shifted from words and eyes to hands and bodies, the oneness would melt them into passion. They made better love after those talks than any other time. "Yes, sir," he said. "We could use some loving." He looked across at the picture of James Darren which hung on the wall opposite the bed. His Victorian ancestor wore a long, dark-brown beard and a black suit. The painter had made the eyes look straight out. "Sorry," Howard said. "I didn't mean to include you."

He weighed again the patience and effort before they would feel close, wanting to get Sylvia in bed. "Nothing wrong with that." He looked at the picture. "Do I see the hint of a smile behind those beady polygamist eyes?" he said to the picture. "Are you trying to say that after living with three wives at once, you think my problem is insignificant?" He put on his slippers. "Having one wife is what makes it significant."

His mother as far as he knew had never treated his father to arbitrary silence and coldness. Sylvia looked like the younger pictures of his mother, the same dark hair, the same thin body. But he couldn't picture his mother reading forever or getting into moods that lasted for days; she was too busy. If she had a disagreement with his father she worked it away. He could only remember her active: sewing, gardening, holding a baby, or visiting her friends in town. He waved his finger at James Darren. "The first law of marriage, which every husband must break, is don't compare your wife with your mother." His mother's activity hadn't kept his father from leaving.

Howard knew Sylvia was bored in Rockwood. "I started thinking the work was important," she said after quitting her job selling insurance. "Besides, my brain has started twitching." She had never explained herself clearly.

He looked out the window at his mother's garden plot. In the spring he had tried to get Sylvia to grow some vegetables—replowing the spot, showing her how to dig the earth open, to insert the corn and bean and carrot seeds and to fold the soil back across. He started her then watched her leave with the rows only half done. "What's the good of it?" she said. Afterward he realized that he had been trying to get the house and yard to look as they had in his memory. He shared his insight, and they didn't talk about the garden again.

But he knew one result of his mother's hard work. When his father was excommunicated for adultery, leaving town with Sister Sorenson, their neighbor across the street, his mother had survived. It had been hard for his father. "He's just like John Rockwood," people whispered. His great-grandfather, son of James Darren Rockwood, at the age of sixty took another wife, a young woman, four decades after the prophet said it wasn't celestial marriage anymore. After his parents' separation, his mother's hard work quilting and selling her quilts had kept her sane. If he and Sylvia had children, even that would soften the force of her introspection. Better for him too to have a son or a daughter. The doctor said that there was no apparent reason they couldn't have children. (e) Frustration at not conceiving.

He walked through the kitchen to check the food, upset that she read instead of cooking, that she wouldn't talk, and angry because he let himself be bothered by something so trivial. Tangled and bound, he sat on the sofa across from her and stared at the floor. She glanced over her book at him several times, finally standing. Soon he heard her taking plates out of the cupboard and silverware out of the drawer.

When he followed, putting his hands on her waist from behind, she turned away and set two glasses on the table. "Will Edgar want some?" She indicated the snake skin.

He smiled. "Spirit mice maybe."

"I hear them nights."

He looked at her. "It's getting to you, isn't it?" he said softly. "Living in this old house." Even though they had changed all the yellowed lace curtains and put carpet down on the floors, he could imagine how she might feel: she didn't have the immediate memory of his family and the acquired memory of his ancestors moving through the musty rooms, enlivening them.

She thought. "I'm handling it. We agreed." They *had* agreed and that was her problem. He kept the farm constantly before her: she knew it was integral to what he was becoming.

"Too many ghosts," he said in a wavering voice. His grandfather and his great-grandfather had both died in the bedroom, twenty-five years apart. They had brought his father's body back from California and buried it next to the others in the cemetery. He wanted to be laid there himself.

"We're not alone," she said in the same voice, grinning.

Tonight he knew. Tonight. He could feel her readiness. If he could just keep his patience and humor. They had sacrificed too many days to tension, too many nights of her lying still on her side of the bed.

"I don't know what I'm doing here, but that's something I'll work out myself." She wouldn't yet commit herself to any specific concern. "I'm happy to see you excited about the farm."

He touched her hand. Closer and closer. They were quiet, eating the steaks. Then the sadness settled back, her eyes dropping away to look at the plate. He could see it happening but couldn't put out his hand to prevent it.

"Yes, the farm and house are OK," she said.

He waited. "You didn't finish."

She said nothing.

"Sylvia?"

"Do the ghosts bother *you?*" she said.

"What ghosts?" He stopped eating.

"I mean, I wouldn't want to live in the house I grew up in." She looked at him. "Too many memories. But that's your business. It doesn't have much to do with what's bothering me."

"What *is* bothering you?"

"You asked that already."

"Right."

They waited.

"Howard, what's bothering me?"

"How should I know?" But Howard thought that they both knew. He watched her eyes, waiting, afraid of opening a difference of mind which would be irreconcilable. The truce of not saying was strong between them.

"I don't know either," she said finally.

"So what am I supposed to do? Just put my life on hold until *you* decide how to talk about it?" He wasn't being fair, and she said nothing. "You never get out since you quit your job, except to go to church. I've tried to introduce you to people, help you fit in. Is that it—you don't have friends?"

"They are your mother's friends or daughters of your mother's friends. I've tried to go out to them, and they smile and act friendly, but they never talk to me like they talk to each other." She looked at him. "Don't you see what I mean? Really, what *do* I have in common with them? What kind of life can I have among them?"

"Now we're getting somewhere."

"Not really. Even that is outside." She was retreating again. "It could be managed."

"Have I pushed you to be like my mother?"

"Don't be foolish. In the first place, I wouldn't let you. I thought you understood that. In the second place, I love your mother. You're way off. It's different in Rockwood, no question about that. I'm just not sure that what's bothering me would be any better anywhere else."

"Well, what is it then?"

"I can't put it in words yet. It's all mixed up."

"Sylvia."

She looked at him. "We've been married three years."

He waited, surprised, still sure that being in Rockwood was the core around which any aggravation had built. "So?"

"Sometimes I feel like my body's going blind, like it's no longer a way of touching anything outside itself."

He grinned, then saw it hurt her and stopped quickly. That's what joking can do, he thought—backfire without warning. She changed her expression, eyes wide and spooky. "Sometimes," she rasped, "I feel like one blink and I'll be gone." She rolled her eyes. "Sometimes there's mold growing all over my skin."

"Be serious now," he said softly. "You started to say it."

"I can't say anything yet."

"Just try."

"I did. You saw how well it worked."

"I'm sorry. I'll listen now."

"No. Not now. It's too complicated. It's you and me and the farm and your father and your mother and the town. But it's mostly something I feel from you."

"When then?"

"Don't push me, Howard." She turned away. "Just leave me alone for awhile, if it's not too much to ask."

He stood. "Well, when you figure it out you can tell me." He took his plate into the living room, his patience gone. When she played this game, he felt less loyal. In his anger he thought of his high school girlfriend, Belinda Jackson, now Belinda Sharp, who worked at the feed store. She had worn a shirt open at the collar today. Filling out his order, she leaned forward and he could see where her breasts flattened against each other. She had a full, nearly muscular body. With Belinda watching, he had refused the help of the dock worker and his hand truck and had lifted a seventy-five pound bag of barley under each arm. Driving home, the force of his desire frightened him. He realized that he had taken to finding reasons to go to the feed store, lingering and talking with Belinda. Though he knew that looking and even talking were not fatal, for years he hadn't allowed himself to let his eyes linger on a woman, waiting for her to look up and discover him flirting. That is until the last month. When he leaned across the counter and talked, he remembered kissing her, fumbling as they held each other and touched, awkwardness and fear keeping them from going too far. Now after having made love with Sylvia, knowing the motions of sensuality, he wondered how he could have been so ignorant, so backward. Imagining possibilities now felt much more dangerous.

His father must have watched Sister Sorenson in a similarly intense manner at first. A speculating eye, one which dragged the body with it as it wandered, was the beginning of the path to infidelity. He had seen the pain in his mother's face, and he didn't want to even approach his father's failing. But Howard was curious. How had it happened? What had the two of them thought and done beforehand. "Exactly how are the seeds of adultery planted?" he asked in the voice of a preacher.

"I'm not sure I heard what you said, Howard," said Sylvia from the kitchen.

"I said, you could drive me to drink, you know."

"Not me." She said nothing else.

Finished with his food, he brought the plate back, sliding it into the sink. He put his hands on her shoulders, but she shrugged them away. "No. It has something to do with the way I feel when you touch me, especially the way I feel when you touch me making love."

·······················
A HOUSE OF ORDER

"Is it the way I touch or the way you feel when I touch?"

"Don't be so analytical."

"What don't you like?"

"I don't know."

"Are you being too sensitive about something I've done?"

She looked at him. "My skin often feels dead when you touch it. Something basic is wrong between us."

"I'm sorry."

"Please don't. It doesn't help to be sorry. Something has just changed."

"Your idea of me?"

"Why do I get the feeling I'm not getting through to you?"

"I'll listen now."

"You're just missing me. You're here looking, but you're not really seeing me. Like touching. Yes, it's like the touching. You touch me, but it's mechanical. As if it's not really me you want, but I'm handy."

He felt his neck warming. For some time now he had used Belinda when Sylvia and he made love, borrowing the more voluptuous curve of Belinda's breasts and hips. He had always known that Sylvia and he were sensitive to subtle changes of attitude, but he was surprised to think she had sensed his thoughts.

"I've got something to tell you," he said. He had the idea that, even if his mental sleight of hand only indirectly bothered her, confession would keep them talking.

She looked at him, puzzled.

"I mean I admit it, I sometimes look at other women."

"You what?"

"I sometimes think about the way other women look, when we — you know —." He saw she was laughing.

"Oh. A bonus," she said. "I had no idea we weren't alone. I was thinking more about simple communication. Just getting on the same wavelength or something. Though I doubt it would do me much good if I got on your wavelength in this case."

He smiled, uncomfortable. They were going too quick, and he wanted to slow down, be sure of what was said.

"What's wrong?"

"I don't think it's funny," he said, trying to keep his voice level.

"Oh," she said. "You don't." She stopped smiling. "You really don't like centering on you, do you? As long as you thought it was just me, we could talk, and you could pat me on the head after it's over and we'd climb into bed and forget it."

"I've never said that it's you."

"No, I guess you haven't. It's not me and it's not you." She frowned. "It's sex. Sex is like a magnet or a radio receiver, drawing all our ambiguity and confusion into a single act. Confusion is its territory. But you probably don't want to talk about that."

"Who says I don't?"

She was quiet.

"Well?" he said.

"I need to finish my book."

"Don't you dare. You can't start then stop with me like that. How could you think of it?"

"Watch me," she said. "We talk and nothing else changes and you think it's all right. I want to think and think until I figure it out then we'll talk." She left the room.

He strode out the back door, slamming it. Soon he would lean across the counter at the feed store, which was empty in his day-dream, and put his hand on Belinda. She'd lead him back and they would lie on grain sacks in the musty darkness. They had come so close to sex when they were younger, but he knew he still only had enough courage to manage it in daydreams.

He walked through the orchard and barnyard into the fields; the dark alfalfa, just now blossoming, rustled with the night breeze. He would start cutting Monday. At the ditch he turned left. Walking helped, moving through his alfalfa, which he had made luxuriant by his work. His field, his farm. He had walked here the days and weeks after he had caught his father with Sister Sorenson, soothing himself with the canal and trees he had known since knowing anything. He moved down the path into the next property, Brother Johnson's, where the willows weren't cut and where thick brush grew along the ditch. Remembering that night and what followed stopped him: he determined never to hurt Sylvia, never to destroy his integrity or hurt Sylvia the way his father had hurt his mother.

"Something about the way you touch me," Sylvia had said. Touching and loving in bed was good, approved by God, such sex being foreign in nature to his father's act, but still when Sylvia and he sweated against each other, panting and clutching, he thought of his father moaning over Sister Sorenson and over his mother, rutting as James Darren and John and his grandfather rutted, and Howard was ashamed. Sometimes he filled his head with Belinda so he didn't have time to think, which also made him ashamed. Now walking along the canal, he was ashamed to be ashamed of his natural, physical self. "You are in one hell of a bind," he said to himself. But knowing he was irrational had never helped him, when in the winding down of his emotions after sex, he had to make himself hold Sylvia, make himself even stay in bed with her. "You are a century behind your time, you slug-minded Victorian prude."

When he came to the fence which marked the boundary of his farm, he turned and walked back. A mist, a thickness, had come into his head, keeping him from understanding how to talk to Sylvia. She wasn't in the kitchen, and he saw that she hadn't moved the book from where she dropped it. When he walked into the bedroom, she was sitting naked on the edge of the bed, watching herself in the mirror. Her small breasts sloped forward to the nipples. Her hands lay flat on her narrow thighs. She didn't turn her head.

"I didn't mean that the way I feel is your fault," she said. "It's easier to analyze someone else's problems. I mean me analyzing you." He couldn't understand what she was doing. "Howard, we've got to get rid of this painting." She took it off the wall and stuck it in the closet, shutting the door. "The grim old goat." She turned toward him. "Look at me," she said. He did and felt his body reacting. Resenting his own action, he reached to shut off the light, keeping his eyes on her body, white in the moonlight. He stretched his chest with a deep breath. In the darkness he could watch and make Sylvia's body blur, he could close his eyes, and her breasts grew heavier, her hips curved wider, her eyes became sensual. Though he felt silly, it gave him pleasure thinking of himself holding Sylvia as the cowboy on the book cover did, with Sylvia submissive as the woman was. He stepped out of his pants and took off his shirt, moving toward her. She turned the light on.

"What are you doing?" he asked.

She touched his cheek and looked into his eyes, too close. "Where are you?" She still hadn't covered herself.

He thought about Belinda. Frankness might help. "I told you. I look at other women. Sometimes I think of them too."

"Who are they?"

"They? I don't mean to suggest that there are dozens."

"You don't have to tell me."

But he did if they were to continue. Part of his attraction for Belinda was the memory of early love, the seventeen year old which seemed to glow out of her fuller body. He was stimulated by imagining again how smooth her skin had been then, how her lips had felt moving against his, how it felt to press against her. In his memory their tentative and incomplete approaches toward full sex possessed a dark intensity which he wanted again.

"What do they look like?" said Sylvia.

He opened his mouth and shut it; he looked at her, wanting her in bed.

Sylvia laughed. "You look like a fish," she said.

He glared at her, grabbing his pants and going into the kitchen. "Don't be mad," she called after him. He waited. "You look so silly when you get mad," she called. She was deliberately provoking him. He pulled up his pants. She followed into the kitchen, moving slowly to touch him on the arm, holding her hand there. "Don't be angry," she said. "It makes you too serious. You start feeling like a black hole, and I feel like everything, including me, is going to be pulled into you."

"What are you doing tonight? Playing games? Teasing? What do you want me to do?"

"Nothing, I want you to do nothing."

"I think of Belinda Sharp for one, the clerk at the feed store."

Still naked, she sat at the table near her uneaten dinner. "Oh," she said, stopped for a moment. He sat in the chair opposite, feeling quieter after his outburst. She pointed to the tubular snake skin. "I think it's quite Freudian that you brought this home." She stroked her chin and made her voice deeper. "Now, Mr. Rockwood, just what were you intending?"

He didn't smile. "Don't be so weird," he said. She grabbed his hand and led him, unwilling, into the living room, making him lie on the couch. She left the room, returning with a pad and pencil, wearing the black-framed glasses she had bought to look more like an insurance agent. He glanced toward the front window: they had no close neighbors now, but the curtains were translucent. Someone coming for a visit would get a start. She sat on the edge of the coffee table. Frowning, she crossed her legs. "When we're making love, what do you think about?" He looked away. "No," she said. "Rule number one is you have to speak truly." She touched his hand. "What are you thinking right now?"

"How silly you look."

She slid the glasses down to the edge of her nose and wrote something in her book.

"What are you thinking?" he said.

She turned the pad toward him. "Talking frightens me," it said.

"Why?"

"It's being on the edge."

"Do I scare you?"

She grinned. "Oh, don't hurt me, Mister Punch," she said in falsetto.

"Can't you say anything straight?"

"I guess not." She frowned. "I mean it's frightening being on the edge. But that's better than not talking."

"I know. Talking frightens me because we've been through it before, and I'm worried that it won't change anything."

"What I hate is when we make love and you're not there anymore." She was changing again, jerking toward what was at the core of her mind. "And I hate it when we hedge our talking."

"I'm sorry," he said.

"I guess it's just part of being married for a few years."

"I don't like that either," he said. "It's too fatalistic. As if it's something which will happen to us because it happens to everyone and which no one can control."

"So you think about a specific woman?" Sylvia put her elbow on her knee, supporting her chin with her hand. Howard felt his face turn red. "I think that your thinking about her is more important to you than it is to me. I wish you wouldn't invite her in though."

"Presto chango."

Sylvia put her pencil to the notebook again and watched him. "So you're into large breasts?"

He jerked his face up. "So you're into jealousy?" Sylvia had identified his interest, which was upsetting, but she also made his imagining grosser than he felt it. "I don't think it's unusual to be attracted to breasts." But he knew he was attracted to Belinda, to his memories of their good times together.

Sylvia covered her face with the notebook. Her shoulders shook. For a moment he thought she might be weeping. But then she spoke and it was only a mock whimper. "You're a true cattleman, always thinking about capacity." She giggled again, unstable. "Are you saying that I don't measure up?"

He looked at Sylvia's legs, at the curve of her waist and felt the motion through his groin, still glad despite what Sylvia had said for the tension of a private image. He looked at her eyes over the pad. Suddenly tired of confusion, he longed for a passion strong enough to overwhelm ambiguity. "I can't help it," he said. "I need you."

"Not so fast!" She looked at an imaginary watch. "Your time's not up." She made her voice serious. "Mr. Rockwood, are those breasts the source of your heaviness?" She looked at him and spoke more softly. "The heaviness that's going to swallow us."

He sat up on the couch. Everything had changed again, and he felt the pain of frustration, a sharp tightening. "Heaviness? What are you after tonight?" He frowned, realizing that she was describing guilt. But he didn't think he could explain to her why he felt guilt or why that made his loving thick and clumsy, hurried.

"When we're making love what do you think about?" he asked. He needed to turn it back toward her. Tired of what she had called hedging, he wanted space to gather himself toward an unreserved unburdening.

"How smooth your skin is," she said.

"Is that all?"

"How good it feels to hold you that close."

"Is that all?"

She held the back of her hand to her forehead. "Sometimes — oh, how can I hold my head up — I think about Mick Jagger."

"OK, so I'm an idiot." He couldn't unburden to a chameleon. "Now you've proved that, what next?"

"And sometimes your body clenches and you aren't there anymore. If your thinking of another woman causes that, I hate it." She wasn't smiling now. "Sometimes the touching changes."

"I won't think of them anymore."

"It can't be that easy. I wish you could see that it's more fundamental than morality. Howard, we've made love for three years now. Is it more exciting to think about someone new?"

"I guess so. Easier maybe. I mean — ."

"I don't remember feeling this way in Salt Lake," she said.

He looked at her quickly. "We were newlyweds then." He thought about the way he felt when they made love. "You said that the touching changes. Well when I touch you my whole body changes. I want it to be the same." Immediately he knew he had said too much.

"The same." She was laughing again. "You want your body to feel the same when you don't touch me as when you do?"

He didn't move.

"That might make things difficult," she finally said.

"Stop it," he said.

He waited, ready to leave or turn it into a joke too if she didn't see, but then her face went sad. "I'm sorry," she said.

"I'm going to finish what I was saying."

She nodded.

"I can't look at you," he said.

She said nothing.

"Do you remember our wedding?" He paused. "We held hands walking to the sealing room. The mirrors on each side showed us for eternity forward and backward in purity. It may be trite, but—."

They were quiet. "But it was important to you," Sylvia said.

"Yes. When I let myself go it seems a violation."

"Howard, what we do in bed isn't—."

"Don't lecture me. I know that. But do you think that knowing what I'm doing changes anything? Part of it is Sunday school from when I was a kid. No one means harm, but all they drill is self-restraint, holding back continually. All that women-are-pure stuff, don't degrade their purity—it makes me shut down when we make love." He stopped. "That's only part of it." He thought about his father, how it had been when he had discovered what his father had done. His mother's face was a grim mask when his father was excommunicated. He hated Sister Sorenson.

"What are you thinking about now?"

"My mother," he said quickly.

"Your mother?"

"She didn't deserve it."

Sylvia said nothing.

"I mean she loved him. How could he do it? I can't comprehend what was in his head."

Sylvia watched him.

"When we make love, instead of you and me clear, forever forward and backward, it's as if he's sitting next to the bed, as if his spirit has seeped out from the floorboards, so he can watch and laugh." He was tired of trying to confront his own captivity. "It would be better if we had a child, if we could make something with our love."

She was quiet.

"No that's not it. Did I make you sad?"

"Yes."

"I'm sor—."

She put her hand across his lips. "It wouldn't change everything if we had children." She looked at him. "Do you think what your father did is unforgivable?"

"Of course not." Someone might forgive and understand.

"I only met your father once," she said. "He was a sad, old man."

He looked at her quickly. "You should have seen him when he was young. He was hard and sharp and strong then."

"Like you?" She smiled.

"What?"

"Do you want to be even more like him?"

"You should have seen him."

"When he was younger?"

"Yes."

"I'd like to see *you* when you were younger."

He smiled.

"I'd like to see you free and simple," she said. "I'd like to see your little boy body. Look inside your little boy head."

"You perverse woman!"

"At least we're getting away from the women with the breasts like pillows," she said. "The ones made for your imagination."

87

"Oh, yes. I'd forgotten."

"Don't lie to me." She held her hands clasped in front of her. "Why do you want to live here?"

"What do you mean?" He was wary.

"What do you get out of it? All it does is remind you of your mother and your father."

"You don't know how good it feels to make this place look right again. I mean when we moved here that field was covered with weeds and brush and crap." He pointed toward the back of the house. "Now, after I plowed the fields, it's filled with alfalfa. I'm fixing the fences, making the barn good again."

"Why?"

"I want it to be like it was before."

"Why?"

"This could go on forever." He thought. "This town is named after my family."

"I know."

"I want people to see the farm like it was when my grandfather ran it and like it was when my father was young, before he left."

"Oh." She turned her face sharply away.

"What's wrong?" He could see she was angry.

"I thought we came here because you wanted to farm."

"I do want to farm."

"Right." She slid to the edge of her chair.

Had she softened her voice and attitude, finally talking to him, only to persuade him to leave? Everything was falling apart again. "I don't understand why you're so angry," he said.

"I came here with you, away from any chance I have of living the way I want to live, to this farm because I thought it was of itself important to you, not because you were trying to prove something." He felt dragged back through the last hour of struggle, as if the pain of opening had been worth nothing.

"It's more than just proving something."

"Is it? Whose idea will you change? You once told me that everyone in town thought your father was like John Rockwood, that they all looked down on your father. Who told you that?" He was silent. "Who did you hear say it?"

"I could see it in their faces."

"You just thought you saw it. Was what your father did so important that they are going to spend all that time worrying about it? For years after it happened? And if the bad Christians among them do remember, do you really think that anything can ever change their minds?"

"I could." She had known all this already, was only now putting it in this desperate light.

"You take yourself seriously. If that's what you want to spend your life doing, fine, but do you think any rational woman would want to stay with a husband whose highest desire is to live someone else's life?"

"You're twisting it now, making it more than it is." He thought about her, asking him leading questions, playing a game with his emotions. "I don't know what you're trying to do, but whatever it is, it isn't working."

"I'm trying to help you see what's happening to me."

"You're pushing me into something. I can't change magically at your demand." He remembered that earlier he could have taken her in his arms, loving her. He hated her for trying to make everything straight first, for having to talk first.

"Mr. Rockwood," she said. "Tell me more about your father."

"Go to hell." He stood. "I won't take any more of this perverse game. Why can't you just say what's wrong like any normal person? I hate it." He finished dressing and walked through the living room and out the front door, slamming it behind him. He saw through the curtains that she didn't move. She thought he'd walk around for awhile then come back like an obedient animal. He knew he was angry, but he had tired of the talking and talking without coming to any conclusion. If her plan had been to force him to a choice, then her plan was backfiring. "Ahhhhh," he shouted in the front yard.

Climbing into his pick-up, he sat behind the wheel, growing tighter and tighter with anger, his body clenching as he thought of the ways she tried to entangle him in her twisted emotions. He felt like smashing his hands through the windshield, cutting himself, anything which would release him from the confusion which she and his own history had conspired to weave for him.

Starting the engine, he jerked the vehicle out of the driveway, driving too fast toward town. His first thought was of Belinda as he determined to make a violent break with Sylvia. He turned down the road to the feed store. It would be closed, but because she had complained about it two or three times when they talked, he knew Belinda worked late every Saturday totaling the books. Feeling a rush of adrenaline, he wanted to see what could happen if he actually approached her. From the top of the road, he saw a single light. No one was at home in the house opposite the feed store. No other building was on the street, and Belinda's car was the only vehicle. Though he couldn't see her yet, he thought Belinda was inside working. Light-headed, astonished at what he was doing, he parked his truck to the side of the building, hiding it behind a low tree.

He climbed out, hesitating with his hand on the truck door. Having read about cowboys approaching their women and having thought that kind of masculinity silly, he still felt an aggressive power inside. Conscious that he was shattering boundaries, he climbed the stairs, striding across the cement dock which went all the way around the building. He paused at the side window, standing back in the darkness, shielded by the nearly closed venetian blinds, and watched her work. She hurried, moving her fingers rapidly over a calculator. He watched her waist and hips as she moved across the room and lifted the top bag of a stack of yard fertilizer to check the tags. He admired her motions, a strong, sure woman, and he realized that she would never be as passive in reality as she was in his imagination. She returned to her desk without seeing him. He waited, trying to figure what to say. As he watched her work, a quieter feeling, another way of proceeding, came to him.

If he was careful, if he talked tonight, touched her hands after the talking, moving slow the way he did with Sylvia, he might actually have her. The same physical motions that worked with Sylvia could work with her. He would have to be kind and tender, the same way Sylvia needed him, another way of touching than the wild and aggressive bouts of passion which had filled his daydreams. They could approach person to person, two people who cared, equally strong. He remembered seeing his father's hand on Sister Sorenson's cheek. Despite his years of anger, Howard knew that his father's sin might have been one not merely of lust but also of humanity.

He walked to the front. Belinda looked up startled as he tried the door, which was locked. She smiled, moving around the counter toward him, opening for him. "Howard Rockwood, what are you doing here?"

He went inside and his imagination failed him: he didn't know how to talk to her out of either vigor or humanity. "I need a bottle of penicillin," he found himself saying. "I remembered you said— ah—that, sometimes, someone is here late."

She walked to the fridge and got out a box. "You're lucky I was here," she said. "Did you use the other one already?" He had forgotten that he had bought a bottle that morning. He took the offered penicillin, brushing her fingers.

"Yes. I mean, no." He hesitated. "I mean I'm lucky that you're here. I wanted to talk to you."

"About what, Howard?" She looked around him out the door. "I didn't hear you drive up. Is Sylvia waiting in the truck?"

Howard cleared his throat. "I parked around to the side," he said. "I came alone."

"What are you saying?" She walked toward the counter where he stood, her eyes on him. "Are you all right, Howard?" She stood directly opposite him on the other side of the counter. "You don't look good."

"Sure. I'm fine." He took a deep breath. He knew they needed to talk, but he didn't know what about. "You have a lot of work, don't you?"

"I'm almost finished for the night," she watched him, apparently curious.

He held up the package. "Do you remember when you helped me give my show calf a shot?"

She shook her head, then smiled. "Yes, I do. You held the rope while I jammed the needle into his butt. He jerked you onto your face in the manure."

"You helped me take my shirt off."

"Then I sprayed you with the hose."

"You came almost every night to help me."

"I came to make out with you behind the shed. Didn't we have fun!"

"Yes," he said, watching her eyes, trying to communicate his feeling.

"Why are you here?" she said. Her face was closed but with a smile behind her eyes. He felt his neck flushing.

"Ah . . . ," he said. She folded her arms across her chest. "Sylvia and I are having a fight, and – ."

"You're having a fight?"

"Things haven't been going well for a long time. It's not working with her."

"And you came to your old friend for advice." The smile behind her eyes was more obvious.

He tried to smile back. "I needed to get away from the house."

She turned toward the papers. "It's a lonesome world, isn't it?" Her voice was flat. She moved away from him, her head up, moving with proud motions as she leaned back in her chair, her hands behind her head. She watched him without evidence of emotion. "I'm full of advice." Her face was veiled firmly now, nearly hard, and he doubted his imagined modes of proceeding, doubted that he had ever seen warmth in her face. "You shouldn't have come down here."

He searched her face again for the inviting smile he thought he had seen that morning, unable to find the seventeen year old behind the weary eyes and thicker face, wondering what he had seen and felt, finally deciding that he had been tricked by the intensity of his memory. She clearly didn't care for him in the way he had imagined for the past month, and he believed he had mistaken the seriousness of his own emotion. Even if he made his motions and voice persuasive, nothing would work. He remembered the awkward hesitation and bumbling of his adolescence, the confusion which he had tricked himself into repeating.

She now retreated even further behind her mask. "I need to finish these and get home," she said. "My husband's expecting me."

"I'll take this anyway," he said.

As he left she turned back to her work. His face and neck burned with foolishness. He couldn't order his splintering impressions, couldn't bear to think of the haphazard selfhood created by what he did and thought. He felt his essence dissipating, reforming itself outside his control. Driving up onto the flat, he looked down on the fields and houses of Rockwood, over which the souls of his ancestors brooded. Five generations of them had spent their lives fumbling and groping for a bright and vigorous intensity, a marriage of spirit and matter, which no doubt would continue to entice and elude. The lights of his house showed where Sylvia waited, perhaps still watching out the window. After waiting uselessly for some gift of clarity, he started the truck and drove home.

She was dressed when he came in. "Well if it isn't Boomerang Bob." Her voice was strained. "Where did you go?" she said softer. Her lips were firm, her eyes wide and frightened. "I feel like such an ass for laughing at you."

He said nothing; his head was spinning.

"Where did you go? You've been gone a long time."

93

"I went nowhere."

"I don't believe you."

"I went down to the feed store." Her head turned sharply away. "And nothing happened."

"Why don't I feel convinced?"

"Belinda was there, working late." He stopped talking. He had seen Sylvia's face totally open, ready to be hurt by what he would say. Despite her clever talk she had never prepared herself for the possibility of him actually being unfaithful. Talking, he had felt pleasure in a kind of power over her, and more than that—a heightening of emotion, telling her about how he nearly made it with another woman. He shook his head, his mouth turning down bitterly. "It's hard for me to talk about it." Then he looked up, seeing from her face one reading of what he had told her so far, and he knew he had to tell her everything, no matter how it made him feel.

"I didn't intend to go there."

"But?"

"But I ended up there. She was working late and—"

"Sounds like what I've been reading today."

"—and then we talked until it was clear that there was nothing but old memories between us. You didn't know this but we dated in high school. After we made each other depressed and embarrassed, I left."

He could see she thought there was something else. "I could see how my father could have gone ahead, where I couldn't. I just made a fool of myself."

She watched him, uncertain, then he saw her decide to believe him, without understanding. "Did you do this to scare me?"

"Do you think I'd—." He looked at her. "I don't know why I left. I'm not trying to hide something or be someone I'm not. I scared myself." They were silent. "What now?" he said.

"I don't know."

"I had the feeling of what I want—something unusual, intense like a vision. I can't say it. Something better and stronger than what we have. Not just a sexual experience, something beyond that. Sometimes I feel that if I could drop my head away, clear out everything that I've been and start over it would be all right."

She smiled. "My romantic Howard, stuck in the here-and-now." She looked up with tears in her eyes. "Isn't that the hell of it?" He moved closer, and she held his head, his cheek against her breast, and rubbed his neck. Soon he felt quiet.

"That feels good," he said.

"Remember when I first saw you?"

"Yes." He recreated the lawn, the trees around the university, the crisp, brick buildings. He remembered her legs, hair, and face, the way she had acted as she spoke to him. "I sometimes think it was worth it." She bent and kissed him, moving her lips harder against his. He shut his eyes, thinking of her then, the way she had appeared to him years earlier.

"Uh-uh," she said. "No way." He opened his eyes. "Look at me," she said. He saw the way she smiled, a flat line, her eyes that had gone through time with him, clear as they had ever been. Her hands were around his shoulders, soft across his back under his shirt.

"Howard," she said suddenly.

"What?"

"You were going away again."

He moved away and sat on the chair.

"Come back." He did. "I like it when you're tender with me." She said it quietly, more as an invitation than a reprimand. "I like it when you're fast, too. I just don't like it when you make me invisible. When you shut your eyes, and I feel you going away from me."

"What now?" He faced her. "You've told me you don't like the way I make love. What else can I look forward to?"

"Howard."

"Maybe I can concentrate on unbuttoning your shirt," he said, doing so. "Maybe I can live in the here-and-now by focusing on taking my pants off."

"You silly fool," she said, looking at him full as he felt the thrill downward through his body. She put her arms around his neck and kissed him. He let her pull him after her onto the floor. She kissed him harder. He touched his lips to her hair, brushing his fingers across her skin when he felt himself slipping away. Moving, he watched her eyes, the speckles of gray across her irises, made his lips touch the texture of her hair, attended to her legs wrapped around his legs, her hands holding tight to the back of his neck, her lips on his neck, made himself feel the warmth and moisture inside her body, sensed his own body straining toward comprehension of the gifts which she lavished on him and which he waited and waited to return to her.

Afterward he wanted to sleep, to cave into himself, alone. She pulled him to his feet. "Come on," she said. "I'm hungry."

"Now I like that. I cook you dinner, you don't eat it, but now you're hungry."

"I'll make some cinnamon toast and lemonade."

He took his robe from the bathroom. "Do you care if I slip into something more comfortable?" he said.

"Whatever you want. But you have to admit, being naked kept you humble for a minute."

While the bread was toasting, they sat at the table. "What do you think about when you're making love?" she said.

"How smooth your skin is." They smiled.

"Howard, I need to go to school."

He looked up surprised.

"I need it as much as you need this farm." She watched his face carefully. "I don't want to thrust us back into the argument. I'm just trying to let you see me."

"You could drive in to Salt Lake."

"It's eighty miles." He saw she had considered it.

"That's a long way to drive everyday."

"Yes. It's too far." She smiled. "I guess that makes it a question of primacy of need."

She had come at length back to what she wanted. He thought about his dream for the farm: making it so that people would pass and say, "Those Rockwoods are fine people. Look at that." It was a stupid dream compared to what she offered. "I can stretch only so much in one night," he said anyway.

"Talk about it tomorrow."

"Sure," he said. "Tomorrow."

She looked at him. "Let's leave it, Howard. Let's sell it and go to Bolivia or Australia with the money."

"You're serious," he said. She laughed. "You're really serious."

"Forget it," she said. Tears stood in her eyes. "I'll be with you." Then she looked away at the snakeskin. "What's your real reason for bringing this home?"

"I've only seen one before."

She laughed again, silvery clear.

After running down the hall to the bedroom, she came back with small bottles of oil paints. She began painting the ribs of the snake; red, violet, and blue building into rings. He watched, smiling and rubbing both hands across his face. She sat naked in the old kitchen with the china cups hanging widemouthed behind their glass doors, her breasts moving back and forth as she painted the green and yellow circles.

Something was falling away from him again, more dead air moving backward, dropping away. He held himself tight, frightened at what was being lost. He looked around at the familiar kitchen where his family had cooked, prayed, and eaten for generations. Now frowning, he pulled the robe closer around his body.

THE LAST
WONDER
OF Nature

Mary Ellen and Spencer stood in Benjamin's doorway. He lay on the floor, his arms folded across his chest, his neck kinked against the baseboard; he wore one or another of his black T-shirts: Scorpions or Guns 'N' Roses or Poison.

"In the morning then," she said.

"What?" Benjamin removed the headphones of his Walkman. His eyes swung from Spencer to her, then back. "What'd you say?" Even across the room she heard the tap and squeak of the song.

"Remember?" said Spencer. "Tomorrow. The big hole in the ground."

"A hundred million years of strata," said Mary Ellen. She watched Benjamin's mouth and eyes. "A hundred million years of erosion." A hand-lettered poster above the bed said, "Skate and Destroy."

"In the morning then," said Benjamin, with her exact inflection, but dragging his tongue across the words, slurring them. She traced the lines of childhood in his face — disappearing, overshadowed by adolescent features, foreign, angry, as if the teenager had swallowed the child.

"We'll travel up the Mogollon Rim," said Spencer, "6,000 feet in a hundred and fifty miles: Arcosanti, Lake Montezuma, the Coconino Plateau, Kaibab Forest. Remember?"

"Bennie," she said. "You promised."

"It's cough medicine," said Benjamin. "Nothing to get anxious about. I had a summertime scratchiness of the throat."

She looked at the thin line of his mouth, which, without smiling, threw in her face some borrowed phrase. "You're mocking me again, Bennie," she said, and Spencer pulled her backward out of the doorway.

"Not tonight," he said. "Let's not get into it tonight."

While Spencer showered, Mary Ellen sat on the counter of the sink. "We've been through it all before," she said.

"I can't hear you."

"He'll grow out of it, like we did."

"We all need a distraction." He combed his hair, the towel loose around his waist. "If we're lucky, this trip will class with our first one." His smile was sly. He had been eighteen, Mary Ellen sixteen when they first made love. Hitchhiking northward from Phoenix to the Grand Canyon, they had left the highway and wandered through the pines until they found the rim, where they lay on a ledge, her hair trailing into the chasm.

Spencer reclined against the bathroom door, arms folded, hips cool. She hooked her fingers in his towel and pulled him behind her to the bed. "So distract me," she said. After fifteen years of marriage, her passion for Spencer had revived; the reddish-blond hairs on his back, the web between his second and third toes, his eyes which dulled but never closed as they made love. "Do you reciprocate?" she thought.

Spencer turned the pages of *The Tao of Sex and Love*, a guide to male longevity through conserving one's *ching*.

She tongued his ear and imagined a shower of gold inside her. "I want Benjamin to have a little sister."

He showed her the illustrations and they settled on "Dance of the Two Phoenix."

"Phoenicians," she said.

Later, after Spencer was asleep, Mary Ellen lay on her back with her palms flat on her belly, welcoming the guest. She sensed the sperm and egg joining, becoming one flesh, the zygote dividing and redividing into a potential Other, attaching to the wall of her uterus, transforming her body. But the words of her son floated up through the layers of her mind, bobbing and surfacing like the bodies of fish.

On the road, Spencer proposed that they drive around to the North Rim. "Commercialization is less offensive there."

"The big C bought this RV," said Mary Ellen. "You're biting the hand that feeds you."

"I guess I'm just a fool for the good old days," he said. She looked into his face, softened and distorted again by the memory of a more vital time and of her younger flesh, as if she were another woman. They had run away together the fall of 1971, and there had been something even at that late date in the air—freelove, Thoreau, sweet smoke, granola, disestablishment. They had felt that the foundations of a bourgeois regime were disintegrating, its cultural trappings soon to be swept away as if by a strong wind. All God's children would live in harmony. Spencer was a sweet and sentimental fool; the Age of Aquarius was a crock.

"Tom Hayden, Jerry Reuben, Eldridge Cleaver, and J. Gordon Liddy performed at ASU last week," she said.

"You left out Jane Fonda."

"She wasn't invited. Male-menopause Aid they called it."

Mary Ellen watched as the pines and meadows of northern Arizona passed the window of their recreational vehicle. The trees grew straight as pillars, strong, as if their roots were in a different world than the one she inhabited. If one believed the myth of wilderness, then the starkness of the prairies, buttes, and canyons might rejuvenate the three of them.

Benjamin fiddled with his skateboard in the aisle. His shirt said, "Nazis for Nihilism," in yellow-green letters.

In Flagstaff they visited a museum: the Native American Through the Ages—wax mannequins, computerized mechanical models, and movie clips. They saw Anasazi Man, Chingachgook, Sacajawea, Dustin Hoffman in Souix drag. A poster showed Pocahontas pointing like Uncle Sam. "You are the next Third World." In her off hand she held a tomahawk which dripped red.

On a table stood a mechanical raven, the size of an eagle. "I will fight no more forever, Honey," said the raven, winking at Mary Ellen.

As they traveled Benjamin locked himself in the bathroom. When he came out Mary Ellen saw that he had shaved his head bald except for a long twine of hair. "We are ashes of the phoenix," he whispered. She smiled, allowing him latitude. She thought he looked like a young Hare Krishna.

Near Bitter Springs the earth was white, yellow, and gray, unhealthy mounds the shape of ant hills marked with vertical cracks. Large steel grasshoppers bobbed up and down, black with their own spit.

"A wonder of nature," said Mary Ellen.

"Surreal," said Spencer.

"Post-apocalyptic," she said.

"Where're the Indians?" said Benjamin.

"Hiding behind those bushes. If we stop, we'll be ambushed."

"A whole tribe of them will circle our RV."

"With nubile maidens in their train," said Spencer, "as a reward for the brave warriors and captives." He looked for a response from Mary Ellen. She kept even her eyebrows still. A sweet and adolescent fool, she thought.

"They'll shoot flaming arrows into our tires," said Benjamin. "They'll shove Molotov cocktails up our exhaust pipe. They'll cut our foreheads and abdomens with stone knives. The flesh will show white for an instant before the blood comes."

"He's going to become a surgeon," said Spencer.

"I'm not sure that what we have here is a surgical impulse," said Mary Ellen.

"Fear and anger are necessary emotions," said Benjamin.

"Axl Rose is a hedonist not a nihilist," she said.

"Nobody's perfect," said Benjamin.

As they passed a dried-up creekbed, a traffic sign on wheels blinked in the middle of the road:

$$= = = = >$$

Spencer turned off in the direction of the arrow but instead of a detour they found a row of Navahos, boys and girls, men and women, selling beads. The booths were constructed from cardboard, gray plywood, and ragged cloth.

"What is a trip without a memento?" said Benjamin.

Spencer backed the RV around, ready to leave, then he shut off the engine. "The beads are plastic and the blankets are made in Mexico," he said, "but I'm easy."

Mary Ellen approached an old Navaho, who sat behind two barrels on which a bead-covered board had been laid. The old man seemed asleep, but when they walked toward him, he stood and shuffled back and forth behind his jewelry. He was shorter than Mary Ellen, child height, thin of body but fat in the face. In the eyes and forehead he resembled Mahatma Ghandi, in the mouth, Robert Duvall. A strip of cloth, midnight blue, held his white hair in a bun at his neck. He kept his head down and moved his mouth, frowning at her.

"Have we met before?" she said.

He looked up, his mouth inscrutable. She examined the beads. "C.C., 1492" was printed on a tag attached to each necklace. "They been in my family long time, but you can trade to get them back, white woman," said the Navaho. Mary Ellen frowned at the small, makeshift tents. "Hand-made Indian jewelry," the sign said. Behind the booths was a mud hogan. In a corral rested a herd of emaciated goats. To one side a young man in a tank-top, apparently the old man's son or grandson, chanted and beat on an oil drum, cut in half. Mary Ellen recognized fragments of the New World Symphony, triple-time, ironic. He didn't smile and his eyes were as angry as Benjamin's.

Spencer removed a bill from his wallet and laid it on the board. The old man looked at it, scratching himself behind one ear. "I had hoped for deed to prime timberland," he said.

"Sorry, I'm fresh out." Spencer put down another bill, then two more. The old man placed the money in his shoe and handed Benjamin a string of beads. Spencer moved to another booth where a young woman in a velvet blouse and tight levis sold blankets.

"Thank you," said Mary Ellen to the old man. "Do you make enough from this booth to live?"

He moved his lips.

"What?" said Mary Ellen, unsure whether the old man had mumbled or had only cleared his throat. "What?" She bent forward and looked into his eyes. The hair rose on the back of her neck.

She jerked her head in a sign to Spencer. Then she gripped Benjamin by his shoulder, and they backed toward the door of the RV. When they were safe inside, Mary Ellen let her breath out. "Crazy as a honker," she said.

"Didn't have all his beads, did he?" said Spencer.

While Spencer drove, Mary Ellen rested on the couch, wondering what filled his head when they had sex. "Froth," she said. "Balloons and ocean froth. Heaving."

What?" said Spencer.

She lay her arm across his shoulders. "I love you when you're vacuous," she said.

She looked into the back and discovered that Benjamin had quietly carved slogans in the paneling of the R.V.: "Night is Light," "Riders of the Storm," and "Anarchy is loosed upon the world."

"You have once again exceeded the limits of propriety," shouted Mary Ellen.

"Thank you," said Benjamin.

"And your ideas suck," she said.

"You don't understand," he said.

"Neither do you," she said.

"So we're even."

Her head felt as tight and multilayered as an artichoke: she walked back to the little room for an aspirin. When she opened the door, she found the old Navaho sitting cross-legged on the toilet seat. "*Ya'at'eeh*, Honey," he said. In his lap lay a buckskin pouch, fist-sized.

"Good lord," said Mary Ellen. She shut the door, a reflex action. Then she jerked the door back open and grabbed his hand, trying to pull him out.

"So, sof," he said, patting her hand. "You very kine, white woman." Mary Ellen found her face close to his. His breath was sour, his eyes rheumy, his hand tremulous.

"We're keeping him," said Benjamin. "He's found a new home."

"You'll have to leave," commanded Spencer, who had turned to look over his shoulder.

"Watch the road, you damn fool *bilagaana*," said the old man. "I don' wanna die young."

Spencer pulled to the side and walked back. The old man stood and dropped his pants. "Excuse me," he said as he shut the door.

"As far as the lodge," said Spencer to the door. "No farther. Do I make myself clear?"

"Yo, Honey," said the voice from inside.

After parking they strolled along the walkway above the canyon. The red and shades of red faded below them.

"You shouldn't have encouraged him," said Spencer.

"I wasn't the one who bought the beads," she said.

"I wasn't the one who got friendly."

"He probably just needed a lift."

But when they returned for lunch, he was still waiting on the toilet. As they began eating he shuffled out and squatted next to the table. Benjamin threw him a few scraps. "He won't be any trouble."

"Pennies a day," said the old man.

"He can help around the place," said Benjamin.

"I do all kines of work: divining, purifying ritual, chants against enemy. I have great knowledge. Like the four signs of danger. Ringing in ears, itching nose, noise in throat, and prickling of skin."

"See how we need him," said Benjamin. "I've experienced all of those."

They stopped again near the shanty booths at Bitter Springs. "What air!" said Spencer loudly, walking around the RV with its door left ajar. "What a life, living out here in the open."

The old man didn't budge.

"Sarcasm doesn't do anything for him apparently," said Mary Ellen.

Spencer drove with one hand, glancing at Emily Post's book of universal etiquette, chapter heading, "Among the Displaced." He turned half-around. "We must be firm but gentle," he said.

Back in Phoenix Spencer locked the old man out of the house. "He'll be gone in the morning if we don't feed him."

"We've already fed him," said Mary Ellen.

"HAAYAAaaYEEYAAaa," the old man chanted against their back door, beating on an inverted garbage can. She heard Benjamin's voice, slightly more shrill: "HOOYOOooHEAHEAYAAaa."

What else could she do? She spread a camping blanket on the floor of the furnace room and led the old Navaho down by his forearm.

"*Ha'at'eesh shinanina?*" he said. "This my room, Honey?" He appeared very weak: she hoped he wouldn't sicken before they could urge him on his way.

"You can sleep here," she said, her mouth close to his ear. "You'll be fine. It's the coolest place in the house. I often bring a blanket down for a snooze myself."

"You the kinest *bilagaana* woman I ever know. *Ahe'he.*"

Mary Ellen forced a chair against the doorknob. "He peed already," she whispered. "He has no reason to come out until morning."

"Feeding him was more than enough," said Spencer.

"The voice of common sense," she said. "You didn't do any better."

"We've been snookered," said Spencer. "A ninety-year-old con man." He placed his hands on her hips. "Let's try out the new blanket." He pointed upstairs with exaggerated motion of his lips, the way the Navaho had. "She said that First Man and First Woman created humanity by working under a blanket made of dew."

"She?"

"The girl I bought it from."

"So you went straight to metaphysics with her?" said Mary Ellen. "You're such a fart." She hooked her fingers in Spencer's collar and pulled him behind her up the stairs.

The old man's chants wove through her sleep, distant, rising and falling on the edge of hearing. She dreamed that the bones of her house moaned and twisted.

Near morning Benjamin shouted. She didn't understand his words, but because of the urgency in his voice, she rushed from her sleep, dragging the sheet halfway to the door before she could disentangle herself. "Spencer!" she shrieked. "It's Benjamin." From the corner of her eye, she saw Spencer roll to the floor, spread-eagled, and extend his arms under the bed.

Benjamin knelt on the landing, looking out at the broad leaves of a corn plant, tall as his face. His sprout of hair was tied with a narrow ribbon, midnight blue.

The old man squatted on the kitchen bar, beating on a cookie tin and singing:

"HAAYAAaaYEEYAAaaHOOYOOooHEAHEAYAAaaYE EYAAaaYEEYAAaaHEEYAAaa."

"He's out," said Mary Ellen. "The son of a bitch got out."

"I thought at first it was plastic," said Benjamin. He reached forward and brushed his wrist across the dried edge of a leaf. A line of red grew from his white skin. The seed clusters drooped, thick with yellow pollen; the ears sprouted pale silk.

"We should have called the police," said Spencer. He shifted a baseball bat from one hand to the other. Mary Ellen rushed down the stairs, her legs shaking from fear and anger. Her muscles resisted motion, and she tripped on the last step, rolling to the floor.

The roots, pale green fingers, gripped the burgundy carpet. The camping blanket lay in a heap, looking like a small animal curled, sleeping or dead. Above her Benjamin broke off an ear of corn, and the plant grew another. He peeled back the husk and showed her the fat, red-violet kernels bursting out of the cob. She lay with one cheek against the carpet, wondering if her limbs were whole. She smelled perfume from the carpet's last cleaning and the sweet, green scent of corn.

The old man climbed down from the counter and sat crosslegged near the dishwasher. "Priddy gut, hey?" he said, pointing with his lips toward the plant. "I sing powerful song." He showed his stump teeth, pulled his lips back in a coyote grin. A sand painting of black, yellow, blue, and white people, tall and thin as corn plants, covered the kitchen tile.

"What are you doing?" said Mary Ellen.

"I purify your house. Purify your *bilagaana* body. You feel like new woman."

"I don't want to feel pure," said Mary Ellen. "I want *you* to leave."

"How you think I feel, you talk like that?" He dipped in his leather pouch and dribbled blue powder from between his thumb and finger, pinched. He chanted:

With black corn flour I make his feet like roots,
With yellow corn flour I make his arms like leaves,
With blue corn flour I make his head like tassel,
With white corn flour I make his penis and jiz bag.

Benjamin walked to the old man and sat cross-legged. A small pottery bowl on the floor held three gray-green buds. The old man used a short, fat stick to grind the buds into paste. Benjamin held out his hand.

"You little white man, you think you steal this too?" The old man licked the paste from the end of the stick. Benjamin looked down at the squat bowl. The heavy seed clusters brushed the ceiling, dipping and swaying, triangular like the heads of rattlesnakes. The old man stirred the paste and licked the stick.

"In the first world lived mist creatures. White mist and black mist come together and make First Man. Blue mist and yellow mist make First Woman. They escape that world through hole in sky. They pass through four worlds. Each world different, each world change them: mist *dine'e*, insect *dine'e*, man and woman with hard bodies and claws. In third world they see flood coming and they climb up inside of reed. They climb rilly high, up through hole to this world. When we climb to next world, everybody live together without fighting."

Benjamin walked from the kitchen to the living room lifting his feet high, as if he continually missed the first in a run of stairs. The corn stalk thickened and grew horizontally across the ceiling toward the upper hallway. "This world is junk," said Benjamin as he ascended the stalk. "Burn it to ashes." The centers of his eyes were black velvet, the size of pinheads. The corn plant suddenly bowed under his weight, and he looked like a possum hanging from its mother's belly until he dropped to the floor.

The carpet stretched then ripped suddenly, a sound like the screech of a panther. "Enough," said Spencer, striding toward the old man, who stood. A button popped, and oranges, bananas, and bread fell from his shirt.

"Whoops," he said. "I been indiscreet."

"You can keep the food," said Mary Ellen. "What else do you want?"

The old man looked up, working his lips.

109

"We'd like to make it convenient for you to leave," said Spencer.

"A horse and two, three virgin gir's would be handy. An' a new black hat."

Spencer took out his wallet. "Let me be as clear as possible. I will pay you to leave. I'll make it worth your while to get out of here. We won't even charge you for the damage." Spencer laid the green bills in a row. The medicine man watched and then rose to gather several ears of corn, which he also stuffed in his shirt. Returning he laid the red and purple ears opposite the bills. He grinned at Spencer, then dribbled more powder from his pouch.

"All right," shouted Spencer. "I've given you your last chance." He grasped the old man by the shoulders and pulled him up. Mary Ellen scattered the painting with her foot. Plugging in her vacuum, she looked the old man in the eye and moved the sucking tube toward the foot of one of the fractured corn-people. The old man moved back; the particles danced on the floor and then flew into the mouth of the tube.

"What do you think of that?" she said. The old man watched as the tube sucked a blue leg and a yellow head. Soon all the figures were gone. Then she waved the hissing tube in front of his face. "I'm not going to let you jerk us around anymore." She threatened his pant leg before shutting off the machine. Spencer emerged from the garage with his power saw.

"You one fierce mama," said the old man sadly. "One powerful witch." He retrieved his leather pouch and shuffled up the stairs followed by Benjamin.

"We may be in luck," said Spencer. He plugged in the chord and tightened the blade guard in its widest position. Then he cut the corn plant off close to the roots and splattered yellow-green corn matter across the carpet. As the plant fell, the leaves swept across the ceiling, rustling like the feathers of a raven.

"Good-bye cruel woman," said the old man from the landing.

"Benjamin," she said, running after them.

110

The door to the bathroom was shut. "Oh, no," she said. "What

next?" But when she jerked it open, she found no one inside. The
the window was open, the screen hung in shreds. She saw a foot
reach and then reach again for a hold above the frame; then it disappeared. "Skaters unite" was written across the mirror in eyeliner.

She ran down the stairs and into the yard. Benjamin and the
old man sat cross-legged on the highest ridge of the roof. Her son's
face was pale; his hands twitched in his lap.

"You win, Honey," said the old man sadly. "From now on I
stay in my room."

"I wasn't trying to win," she said.

"Don't worry," Benjamin said to him. "You can grow another
one." His speech was slow and slurred. Mary Ellen reached her
hands as if to catch him. If he tried to stand, unsteady as he was, he
would fall off the roof.

"Mebby so," said the old man. "Mebby tomorrow. Mebby
next week."

"You hold still," said Mary Ellen as Benjamin leaned to place
his arm around the old man's shoulder. "Don't move even one toe,"
she shouted. Benjamin bent to listen, his face puzzled, his mouth
slack. "You get him down," she shouted. "He's sick and he's going
to fall."

"Many times," said the old man to Benjamin, "there is a gir'
pining away. Her mother and father or her husband don' know
what to do wi' her. So they organize a three-day sing. They call me
in and I cure her by singing over her and by sucking impurity out
of her body and her breasts. She then whole and clean. Makes me
powerful medicine man."

"Sleight-of-mouth," said Mary Ellen. "A damned fraud."

"Mebby so, *bilagaana* woman." He handed Benjamin the pouch
and then placed his mouth on the boy's neck, working his cheeks.
He removed a piece of turquoise, large as an egg, from his mouth
and threw it down toward Mary Ellen, who caught it in her hand.

"Spencer, get the ladder," she shouted.

"Hey," said Benjamin. "Don't get your hair up."

The old man put his hand to one side of his mouth like half a shriveled megaphone. "Don' worry, Mom," he called down. "Don' get your hair up." He put one arm around Benjamin.

"HAAYAAaaYOOooYEEee," sang Benjamin. In his mouth and chin he looked like Robert Duvall.

Spencer came out with the ladder and leaned it against the house; it didn't reach. He lay it on the grass, and Mary Ellen ran to help him extend it.

Neighbors hearing the noise had come to watch. They looked at Spencer and Mary Ellen struggling with the ladder and then up at the old man sitting with Benjamin in the shade of the towering corn plant.

"Truth is found by leaving a familiar home and going out to meet a stranger," said one neighbor.

"Then the stranger eats you alive."

"You need a longer ladder, Spencer," said a third, more practical neighbor.

Spencer and Mary Ellen finally hooked the latches securely. He climbed to the roof and then stood, watching Benjamin and the medicine man, who took a dark blue stone out of his mouth and handed it to Spencer.

"Priddy gut, hey," smiled the medicine man. He mouthed stone after stone from Benjamin's neck. The old man and the boy laughed as the blue eggs dropped through the air, flashing in the sun.

"Get them off the roof," shouted Mary Ellen.

"Why?" said Spencer. "I can see all the way to the mountains from here." He sat next to Benjamin and patted him on the shoulder. "Good toss, son," he said. Spencer hung his legs over the edge of the roof, swinging them as Benjamin beat time on his thighs. The old man sang:

To yinaa,
To yinaa,
Shi'at'eed bina'adaltsozi,
Ashlaa,

Ashlaa. Spencer sang:
Across the ocean,
Across the ocean,
I made love to a girl
With almond eyes.

Their voices rose and fell in counterpoint. "Male bonding," he said to Mary Ellen.

She observed the transmutation of her son's eyes and mouth; her hackles rose again. She studied the motions of Spencer's legs and arms, the blank and foreign aspect of his face.

"You a lone woman now," said the old man.

"Women!" said Spencer. "I've never understood them."

"What's to understand?" asked Benjamin.

The stones fell like pale seeds onto the lawn and into the up-lifted hands of the people below. "We're cookin' now, Honey," said the medicine man.

Mary Ellen thrust her hands upward, feeling the pulse and texture of the air. Her lips formed the word of potency, and she was on the roof.

Don't ask me how it happened: I was as surprised as she.

JENNY, CAPTURED by THE mormons

I

The pills were white, oval-shaped, a double horseshoe set in plastic. Jenny had eaten the eighth one well before dawn. A week earlier she had told Peter that today would be the first day of her fertile time. He had believed her, and she had watched with pleasure the desire which played across his face, making his smile flat and his eyes dark and hot. He would come to her bed tonight.

Sariah, Ruth, and Ishmael still slept, so Jenny slipped out the front door of her apartment building. Facing west, she walked the margin between the cemetery and the rich houses. I'm surrounded by sleepers, she thought, moving quiet-footed in the shadow of the mountains. She watched outward as the jagged line of sunrise crept across the lake toward her. It lit the haze spread by the catalytic stacks at Kennecott Copper and blazed from the horn blown by the gold-plated angel on the highest spire of the Mormon temple. "By the dawn's early light," she whispered. "Oh, say can you see." Years ago she had lifted a recording of Jimi Hendrix at Woodstock.

The whine of his guitar sounded like bombs falling and exploding. What so angrily he hailed: Vietnam and the rockets' red glare. As if the earth itself had detonated; black, violent Jimi made the strings burn. She was sixteen then, a child of rock and roll, and his guttural songs still released her soul. Janis Joplin, Joe Cocker, Twelve Years After. Nineteen years after.

One hundred and fifty steps past the mausoleum with the eye engraved above the door, she opened her fist and the plastic package of contraceptives, pale as snake eggs, slipped into an evergreen hedge. Her left hand had not known what her right was doing, so only a portion of her mind traced the pills' falling. If she hid them in any secure place, one planned and remembered carefully, Peter would discover them. He believed that any method of preventing birth was abortion.

He had warned Jenny that during the window of her fertility, he would come every night, not his usual pattern. A year earlier he had dedicated all his mind and days to studying the Book of Revelation, memorizing details of the Apocalypse. Before feeling his vocation, he had been stable, sensitive, even doe-eyed. He had filled her house and head with quiet talking. For four years of their marriage he sold children's books door-to-door, moving ten or twelve sets a day, three times the volume of anyone else in the company, he told her. She knew he could have sold plastic diamonds or beachfront property on the salt sea—anything. She had never watched him work, but apparently women opened their doors, looked into his face, and let him in; he weaved them about with words. Suddenly he had quit. "If I traffic long enough in the carnal world I will forget the language of God." Now he stayed away from her weeks at a time studying abstractions: angels, seals, beasts, and thrones.

He was one way then, now another. How to think of the difference? A decay: what had been clear and strong was muddled and weak. A mask: he had put on a fanatic's face, adopted a foreign system of words. A burial: he was child and mother, the old Peter en-wombed inside the new. She pressed her hands to either side of her face. Whatever the confusion of then and now, he had become unreliable.

"You will not stick me with another child," she had thought, not said. She had measured the intervals of her cycle—seven days, seven days, seven, six, twenty-seven days, now twenty-eight with the pills. Peter was determined that they would have a fourth child soon; he felt certain this one would be extraordinary.

"I think not, Peter." She breathed the words. The pills caught in the bush behind her were a joke on him. She grinned. No more fundamentalist babies. She slapped her feet on the sidewalk, a dance of anger.

Turning toward home, she counted in loops of prime numbers—eleven sets of seventeen steps, seven of five, three of three, whispering the words, hearing the tolling syllables. Today it was not rock and roll but numbering which calmed her, and she worried that she was adopting Peter's habits of precision.

Once inside she opened the refrigerator—not enough food for the children, especially with Peter coming. "I'm going on a scavenge," she said to the two girls. "You'll stay with Sister Parker."

Sariah, the oldest, grabbed Ruth. "You want to play with the toys? We'll have fun. Come on." Sariah found her own clothing, then stood on the couch while Jenny dressed the other two. At four Sariah was precocious and imitated the poses of the women on billboards and magazine covers. As Jenny watched Sariah angled her small round hip out, threw her head back. "Learning the ways of Babylon, the movements of the Whore of the Earth," Peter would have said. Not so far wrong. Learning the ways they made women's flesh precious. Jenny wondered that Sariah could mimic so early.

She finished with the baby, who sang and bounced his hands on his fat knees, and pulled them all out the door. She couldn't drive the car because the starter spinned and whined now instead of engaging with the engine, so she carried Ishmael with the girls walking behind through the warming air to the welfare office, where she had been drawing checks since Peter's decision had made him unsteady in love and babywatching.

"I need proof that one of you is actually looking for a job," said Cynthia, her self-sufficiency officer. Her first officer had sensed something wrong in the angle of Jenny's words, had sent investigators, who came on a night Peter was visiting. "Sure, I can take care of her," he had said. Now they wanted her off welfare.

Jenny measured the other woman's response. "Two later this morning. One answering phone orders. This company sells songs on television. All these songs put together on one record. And people call in and order it. I'd take down their numbers." Jenny made her voice deep for Cynthia. The ravages of sorrow and poverty. Opening the tight government fist.

"And the other?"

"It's a flag woman job. Benson Construction." She leaned forward and put one hand on the desk between them. "I've got to pay the day-care woman."

"Get one of your people to watch them."

"Who are you talking about? I have no people around. You know that from our first talk."

Cynthia clasped her hands in front of her. "I'm not supposed to ask this, but are you Mormon?"

Jenny's stomach relaxed: she was in. "No," she said, and Cynthia's face showed immediate sympathy. "I had no idea of what I was getting myself into moving here from Texas." Jenny allowed her words to relax into a down-home drawl.

"Well that might explain your bad luck."

Jenny knew of a dozen places, where if she said she wasn't Mormon, the same angry sympathy would come, and she would be given work immediately. Salt Lake City was like a big high school where the cliques all misunderstood each other and refused to talk. Lucky for me, thought Jenny. I can move between. She had plenty of options if she had wanted steady work away from Sariah, Ruth, and Ishmael.

"Look at this." Jenny opened a small calendar book into which she had scattered times and places. "After all this you'd think I'd get something."

"What do you do when you interview? Do you tell them straight off you're not Mormon?" said the woman. "It's tough to get a job here but maybe an interviewing seminar would help. You can't get a check until next week anyway. You knew that before you came in. And I can't authorize you getting even that check until you have more success with your hunting. There are limits to what I can do."

If I took a job I wouldn't need your foolish head, thought Jenny. You are a house divided against itself. "Thank you," she said, smiling and turning away quickly. Damn you.

She walked her children back nine blocks to her building, where she turned at a right angle and continued for three more streets to the house of the Mormon woman who kept a day-care center. Jenny had allowed herself to be baptized when she first came to Salt Lake. She had understood quickly that she needed to join to get along, and she had studied the Mormons' books for five years. But she still thought of them as the Mormons—the others.

"I have two interviews," she said. Sister Parker was a large woman with graying hair and a wide, flat, sometimes sympathetic face. "One is as a saleswoman in a nice clothing store. The other is a secretary in the church office building. With any luck I'll get at least one of them. I can pay you ten dollars for the two hours I'll be gone."

Sister Parker stared at her. She had tended perhaps seven times for Jenny, and Jenny knew she was always tangled in her mind, caught between pity and anger. The time would come when she would throw Jenny out instead of helping. "It isn't good for you to expect this of me."

"I said that I'd pay you ten dollars."

"And how can I take it? It's like stealing food out of your babies' mouths. You have to get control of some part of your life. If your husband—."

The woman had no idea of control. Jenny allowed the slightest flaring of outrage to show in her face.

"Never mind," Sister Parker said. "Just never mind." She turned to the children, smiled and helped each to find a toy. She talked to them in a voice from which all anger had been carefully drained. You can give to them without guilt, can't you? thought Jenny. Good. They are the ones who deserve all gifts.

One day Jenny had left her apartment with the children sleeping inside. She had laced up a pair of skates she had bought for six dollars from Deseret Industries. Then she rolled out the door, flickering through shadow and moonlight under the branches of the trees, floating like a she-coyote between the tall buildings downtown, free of her children's wants for a space, free of their mouths. But her mind twitched with the idea that the house had caught fire. The motion and the fear of leaving her children were exhilarating. Ten blocks away she panicked and rushed back, thrusting her skates forward so forcefully that she fell several times. Finally she took them off and ran up the hill barefoot. The children were fine, but she clutched their sleeping bodies and found tears coming to her eyes, needy.

Returning to her apartment from Sister Parker's, Jenny put on her house-cleaning clothes. As she rode the bus downtown, she considered the other riders. No use in worrying about the first seats; too close to the driver, who could throw her off.

In the fourth seat a suit and a teenager leaned toward each other, smiling and gesturing. Not relatives or friends, too much tension in their bodies, despite the obvious pleasure in the talking. She frowned. Drugs or sex? They would probably talk of neither one right on the bus. Hands moved in downward angles. "Snowbird," she heard. "Park City." Skiers. It was the fifth of August and they slobbered over talk of slopes and powder. In summer, unless

they found someone whose conversation would carry them forward or backward to winter, skiers walked and spoke like daylight
vampires, stuporous. If it was October, she could say, I need four
more bucks (or fifteen) for a season pass. They would give it without questioning, laying it in her palm which they thought shook
from the urgency of their own habit.

Fifth seat, left. A woman, mid-twenties, in a long dress, puffy
pioneer sleeves. Two children sat with her; two more were fifth
seat right. Fundamentalist polygamist. The woman would have nothing to give, dividing an income with four other wives. When Jenny
had first come to the valley, she had thought that Mormons, funda-
mentalists, and polygamists were factions of one group. Such thinking offended all, a significant mistake. Now Peter had slipped into
the area between. He was fundamentalist but not polygamist, at
least as far as she knew.

The bus moved under an overpass; "Sal liberated Anna here,
July 4, 1987." People made signs everywhere, like wolves pissing
on a bush. "Skiers do it on a hill"—bumper sticker. "Philosophers
do their best thinking sitting down"—university toilet. "Mormons
for a gay priesthood"—mimeographed pamphlet. People talked and
talked.

Sixth seat right was two suits, male and female. The inclination
of their bodies showed little affection. A business, not a flirtatious
contact. Too bad. Desire to impress sometimes opened the pocket.

Seventh, a student, red-eyed, going the wrong way from the
university this time of morning. Probably worked all night. Students would give change when asked. No doubt they gave up their
own lunches, transferred to her children. He would have spent his
already; not worth marking for later.

In front of her hunched two skaters, angry eyes, tight nearly
spastic voices; they were foreign, tufts of colored hair sprouting cra-
zily. The board she could see had names written across it in
fluorescent green and in black. Not a snowball's chance for even a
quarter.

121

Immediately across sat a young man, slacks and shirt, no tie. Not a recognizable uniform. Clerk in a bookstore, maybe; maybe worked in a photography or a crafts shop. A sweet-faced innocent. He would reach in his pocket and give to her, wouldn't use her own obligation of self-reliance as an excuse. "God helps those who help themselves," women said to her, never men. But she couldn't approach him on the bus. Enclosed space would make him feel trapped; he'd tighten-up instead of expand.

The bus stopped and he rose; she followed. Off the bus he took out a sheaf of pamphlets, handed her one. "Look and Be Saved," Salt Lake Baptists. He rushed away, frantic and tremulous at once, solitary, handing salvation to what he thought was an overwhelming ocean of Mormons. He thought himself a stranger in a strange land. Like me, thought Jenny, feeling a sympathy of condition. In another world, I could love that man, she thought. But she had learned from Peter that innocence was unstable.

Jenny walked toward the Mormon temple. She would be ushered away if she worked directly on the grounds, but she might manage a dozen passes between the parking lots and the entrance. As she walked she developed her shuffle, looking people in the faces then away as she jerked her thoughts from pain to pain of her life. If she allowed despair to register in her eyes, people noticed her, gave her money. She thought about the miscarriage, four months along. She considered the fact that her parents were dead to her. They were at that moment slowly growing old in Muleshoe, Texas, but she would never see them again. She worried over Peter's transformation into an obsessed man and her own craziness which came from living with him.

She could sense when she had created the proper amount of distraction and sorrow, too much and no one looked at her, too little and they were suspicious. When she reached that middle place, they felt pity for her. She believed that they gave because she was like a mirror to a weakness hidden inside which could suddenly drag them down to her level.

"I have three children and my husband left me." It worked on women who were shopping or visiting the temple and on men whose faces showed sudden guilt.

"I need three dollars more for bus fare back to Texas," she said to two socially conscious suits. They gave her what they thought was a more effective investment than any overnight house for getting her off the streets.

As she began working she knew herself as a certain woman (bag lady — begging) as if she stood outside her own flesh. But then she was full of herself and felt nothing but the pain. After three hours she was exhausted, but she had ninety dollars and three flyers: a description and street map for the Sea of Salt Refuge Mission; an advertisement for "the development of the beautiful you" — breast implants and proportioning, nose and chin adjustments, tanning, lyposuction for perfection of buttocks, color analysis, "wake unto the new you"; and a pamphlet on a food storage delivery system. She saved the last one because it showed promise of making money. The Mormons' ancestors had been constantly near starvation as they tried to bleed nourishment out of the desert; and every good Mormon still hoarded food. Food neurosis which continued down to the fourth generation. Strong desires could be manipulated, but Jenny hadn't yet figured the mechanics of such a big project.

On the bus homeward she thought about Peter. For years while he was in school, she had left him studying in their apartment as if she was going to normal work. Angry when he finally discovered what she did, he had made her quit. With him gone she had started again: Crashing club meetings, banquets, and conventions at the U, eating and sliding food into pocket bags for the children.

Begging as a deaf person in the university library, confronting students brain-dead from reading who looked up into her mute face and reached in their pockets before they could think. She handed them business cards with the sign alphabet printed on them. "Thank you, thank you," she signed again and again.

Reading meters for Utah Power and Light. She had branched out, suggesting door-to-door that a small contribution in cash could significantly reduce the yearly bill. All her customers felt like they were engaging in a subversive activity against a monopoly. She made seven hundred dollars a week until she began to feel footsteps behind her and moved on.

Collecting donations for a Cub Scout banquet. Peter and the kids had lived on frozen spaghetti and French bread for a month.

Eight months earlier she had bought forty bottles of Mexican vanilla and a pound of powdered Indian corn from a roadside van. She told all the women in Relief Society that Peter's former missionary companion owned a small mine in the mountains outside of Chilpancingo where his great-grandfather had uncovered a cement cavern with paintings of white-skinned, blue-eyed people on the walls. Inside the cavern his ancestor had discovered urns filled with a seed, which when ground made a powder that prevented sickness — "Jaredite flour" Jenny called it. The Mexican's family had eaten small amounts of the powder daily for three generations, and his grandfather still lived — a hundred and twenty years old. Jenny was surprised when only a few doubted her story. She sold the vanilla by the bottle and the powder by the half-ounce, three and forty dollars respectively, with orders amounting to over five hundred dollars.

Jenny's grandfather in Texas had traded horses until he had a small herd which he sold. He used the money to buy land at the bottom of a slough. With a rope, a mule, and a dredge, he dug ditches and lay perforated pipe to drain the swamp, thereby clearing a small farm for himself. Creating a space to live.

But now she had lost her ambition, and she just made enough for her children from scavenging and from moving between state and church welfare. She had an idle plan for stealing a bishops' storehouse order form and reprinting it, but she didn't know exactly where they were kept at church. All the ones the Relief Society president gave her were filled out already, with pen lines crossing and tangling the printed ones.

After the bus dropped her near home, Jenny took a five and
five ones out of her boot and placed them in her wallet. She hugged
her children, opened her wallet, and counted the bills one-by-one
onto Sister Parker's table.

"Keep it," said Sister Parker, stuffing the money into Ishmael's
diaper bag. "Just get one of those jobs."

Jenny smiled at her. "You are a gracious person." Jesus said to
the Gentile woman, let the children of God eat first at the table.
The woman said, yes, but the dogs can eat of the crumbs which fall
between. Then her daughter was healed. And the dogs are filled
while the self-righteous starve, thought Jenny.

She walked to the grocery and spent all the money on food.
On the way out, she parked her cart and left Sariah and the other
kids to watch it. Walking to the back of the store she asked for
cardboard boxes. One of the stockers pointed to a pile, ready for
crushing. She returned to the front along the baking aisle and lifted
two packages of powdered milk and ten pounds of sugar, sliding
them into the empty boxes as she walked. She placed the boxes on
top of her other groceries and left the store.

II

Peter slipped inside the door of Jenny's apartment an hour after
dark. "How many years has it been since we went for a midnight
walk?" he said.

"It's not midnight."

He pulled her through the door.

"What about the kids?" she said.

"We can see our windows from the cemetery." He led her under the trees, the moon glowing from the headstones, his face dap-
pled with leaf-shadows. Once he had been so straight that the sweet-
ness was an excess — a Mormon Boy. Now he reminded her of young
Marlon Brando — compact, intense, brooding. She loved him both
ways. Tonight his black hair shone: *The Wild One*, *On the Waterfront*. She thought of Hendrix's song "All Along the Watchtower."
Waterfront. When she followed on a record the random lilt of notes,

125

she often felt her consciousness float separate from her body. Sariah, Ruth, and Ishmael lay tangled in their bedding. Wa-wa-wa-watchtower. No connection but the sounds. Sariah's kindergarten teacher had taught her the rhythm of numbers, the patterns in leaves, fences, houses, repetition of faces. The regular bass, blue, underneath Hendrix's shrieking guitar. "There's so much confusion." The black-jacket cool of Brando's walk. But that was in the other movie, *The Wild One*. Her mind jerked back: Peter's shadowed face was immobile except for his eyes which remained on her as they walked. Waterfront. White stones lining a rounded shore. A double horseshoe of stones. She flicked her eyes at Peter.

"You're quiet tonight," he said, as he ran one finger along her jaw. That was the danger of letting her thoughts go: his power of intuition. She had allowed her steps to follow those of the morning. The bushes where she had dropped the package was five steps away, and her mind was pulled to the repetition of pills, a doubled row, four sevens, a gap at the bottom. Five were sugar pills. Conception is a sacrament, Peter said to her often. Since he had become unstable, his intelligence sinking further behind his intense eyes, he had referred to sex as procreation. Calling spirit babies from heaven to inhabit bodies, performing God's work, expanding Peter's share of God's glorious dominion. Children aren't children; they are arrows in the quiver of a divine warrior.

"Remember," Peter said as they walked past a fir with branches that touched the ground all around. One night in the first month of marriage they had made love inside its cave. He started leading her in again.

"The children," she said. "I can't be easy about them." She kept his hand and pulled him back to the apartment.

"Complacent, heretical, nosey fools," he said, indicating her neighbors. His voice was hard now. Jenny had warned him to be discrete so she wouldn't lose her church welfare, which she claimed on the grounds that he had abandoned her. He had and hadn't left. "I won't sneak to you anymore," he said.

Even Peter must be controlled. "Don't worry about them then," Jenny said. "I'm tired of lying. It won't bother me if I lose the food."

"I was joking," he said, spreading his lips and grinning at her. "I feel like I'm one of the spies Joshua sent into Jericho before he fit the battle. 'Go view the land, even Jericho. And they went, and came into an harlot's house, named Rahab, and lodged there.' And the walls came a tumblin' down." Jenny looked into his face; she couldn't determine the extent of his irony, but her legs were weak from fear and anger at the sudden change. Now he was a puritanical fundamentalist bastard. His transformations were always unexpected, like the face of her younger brother when she had left for a semester at college and he had changed from sweet child to angry adolescent. Her mother's eyes had become sad, bewildered. But Peter changed instantly, flickering in and out of himself. Jenny felt like weeping for the loss of him, who had been whole once, even if that fullness had been Mormon. What is wrong with you? she said to herself. Pull yourself together. She thought about the pills hidden from Peter. She smiled at the trick on him but quickly dragged her thoughts away again; he was as good a reader of faces as she was.

She lay his food before him and sat across, watching him eat. At first he left her only three or four days, finally a week, at a time. "I've been researching the end of the world," he said. "I feel that someday I can understand what Abraham knew when God showed him every atom during every second of existence from the beginning to the end." She knew he read Revelation with an Old Testament eye—finding dark tangled vision, violence.

At first she had said to herself that his absences made it the perfect arrangement—the occasional pleasures of a man, without any entanglements. But she knew she wasn't being honest with herself. There were ways and ways of entanglement. Fundamental Peter. Fundament. She would not sleep with him at all that night.

Jenny also believed he was as suspicious of her hesitations and avoidances as she was of his absences. She recognized herself as a

127

skilled liar; but until she had bought the contraceptives (which she had done as soon as he began coming and going irregularly) she had difficulty deceiving Peter; whenever she looked in his eyes, secrets dribbled out her mouth. She still didn't trust herself, so she had dropped the pills, half-consciously, poorly hid, where any bitch dog or child could ruin her plans for preventing another baby. If the pills worked on the bitch, there'd be one less litter of puppies to experience sorrow in this world. But Jenny could see the drugs, two rows bent in a tight curve; she numbered the bumps of plastic and received the sensation in her fingers as if she were running the tips across the crowns of her teeth. She shook her head. Three times since he had come, her mind had been pulled back to the pills. She believed Peter knew something was wrong; he had certainly been disturbed by her disturbance of thought. His eyes still followed her, his mouth still frowned, considering.

"I was thinking about that house where I met you," she said quickly.

"Long time ago."

"Not so long. I was drifting through."

"Still a flower child. A decade and a half too late."

"It seems so long ago. We're getting old Peter."

"We're whining old, Peter." He mimicked her voice. "Only five years."

"You took me to a concert that weekend—"

"The singer was homosexual," said Peter.

A new rocker, the old rockers weren't gay that she knew of. That was another borderline she had never crossed. She thought of Jimi Hendrix, Jimmy Morrison, bare-chested, Eric Clapton and his magic fingers, Jack Bruce's silver, sexy tenor. She had heard Jack Bruce on the radio the other day and his voice was ruined.

"Babylon," said Peter. "You are chastising me by reminding me of when I was fully in Babylon. Babylon the Great, the Whore of the Earth." She had a hard time pulling herself back to his talk. Peter wore corduroy pants, a pinstriped shirt, but he slipped into the fundamentalist talk as if he were a southern Utah polygamist farmer. Pitchfork in hand. She sucked in her cheeks, imagining the tight bun pulling her face backward into a frown. Polygamist Gothic: they'd have to widen the frame for the other women.

"What are you doing?" he laughed, and the craziness disappeared from his eyes again.

Jenny remembered him as he was when she first saw him, his eyes clear as they were at that moment. She reached to touch his cheek. "I was wondering why when I unloaded from the bus station five years ago, why I went straight to the university."

"It was destined that you find me."

"I wanted to find someone to live with," she said. "I thought I could find a college student to live with." Jenny had wanted an untrammeled man, a younger James Dean, before the tight and angled face, the experienced eyes. Bring up a man-child in the way he should go, and when he is old he will not depart from it. She hadn't found Peter young enough.

"You chose the wrong place," he said. She had stumbled across a dance at the Institute of Religion. Free food, she thought. She had danced with Peter, had seen in his eyes innocence, depth, and sensitivity, and was reminded of her own pain. They walked home together: he had offered her a piece of apple pie. A line, she had thought — etchings pie, all-American seduction — and she had anticipated watching his eyes as they made love. Instead she found a house full of young men, all younger than her, just returned from their two-year missions, repressing their sexuality until they were married properly in the temple. They gave her the first doctrinal lesson that night, five lay preachers surrounding her, their words made intense by sexual deprivation and by their memories of recent full-time missions in Japan, Belgium, Australia, Tennessee, and California, where they had spent every waking minute bringing souls to God.

"You made me get baptized before you would marry me." She still thought of him as her lover, not as a husband. She had never wanted him to possess much of her, her of him. Now he was as unpredictable as the lover she had wanted. When she first looked into his eyes, she saw sensitivity, not tenuousness. After twelve months of marriage, he began brooding, after four years, he began reading Revelation all day, stewing his brain in visions of monsters, fire, and God.

"I'm sorry," he said. "I had you baptized by a defunct priesthood." She shook her head as she tried to focus. "They departed from the truth in the nineteenth century. The leaders were pure before they disobeyed God and yielded to the demands of men. This city is tight with sin, but they think all is right in Zion." He was more pure than the Mormons, fundamentalist, fanatical. Jenny had the ability to feel someone's meaning as strong as her own thoughts, to invite another so fully into her own head that she forgot who she was; it was disorienting to be unable to follow his words with any empathy. Following completely would bring insanity. "You have never met my father."

"I did once, remember, at the reunion."

"He took me once to the ocean. He just took me out of school one day and drove to Santa Barbara. We slept on the beach because we didn't have enough money for a room. The waves rolled and rolled all night, hypnotic. He tried to talk to me about God. But he couldn't because he never knew him. No one has known God as I do. Not even Moses who saw God in the burning bush. Even then on the beach, I could sense that my father wasn't familiar with God."

Jenny knew that she was an instrument of sympathy. If her power was in hearing words, his was in speaking them. That was why, mismatched, they remained together. She could hear the intense voice of God as Peter spoke. She imagined the numbers of the waves rolling in, three and three and three. But she could also sense his father's quietness, invisible to Peter.

Peter had once been like his father, and she couldn't measure exactly the point of change in him. After her baptism he said, "When we are married we'll pray about every important decision." They had prayed every night and listened afterward for answers from God. Jenny had felt faint stirrings of pleasure as she considered the possibility that a God-father and a God-mother were listening; Mormons believed that even God was married, continually producing offspring. Peter often rose from his prayers with a sour face, saying, "Why doesn't he speak? I have the right to answers." He prayed that they would have strong children; she gave birth to three healthy bodies. He prayed with the rest of the church that a drought would be tempered and then that the floods would draw back.

Finally he came to Jenny. "I've made a decision," he said. "Listen." He read to her from the Book of Abraham. " 'I, Abraham,' and so on and so on, 'having been myself a follower of righteousness, desiring also to be one who possessed great knowledge, and to be a greater follower of righteousness, and to possess a greater knowledge, and to be a father of many nations, a prince of peace, and desiring to receive instructions, and to keep the commandments of God, I became a rightful heir, a High Priest, holding the right belonging to the fathers.' " Peter thought that the bishop should call him in and advance his rank in the priesthood. He told her many times that someone would come soon and call him to be a general authority, an apostle, one who would be the prophet at a time very close to the end.

He decided that his failure came because he was too much like his namesake, Peter. "He was too practical, too forceful, bull-headed. He was too stubborn. How different would the world have been if John had been made the new leader of Christ's church. He was sensitive and loving, visionary." That was when he committed to reading Revelation seven-times-seventy. "The lilies of the field toil not, neither do they spin. God, I can no longer do thy will and work for my bread. I ask them to give us manna." He quit his job but believed that they continued to survive because of his prayers, not because Jenny revived her talents.

131

She looked at him as he ate, past and present images of his face tumbled in her head. I was the manna, thought Jenny. Why have I stayed with him so long?

"I have discovered the secret," he said tonight, looking up from his plate. "Three is a secure number: triangle, pyramid, Trinity. Seven is so much more stable, secure in four dimensions, time as well as space. If I can discover the core word of truth from seven different angles, I can know the Adamic word of truth – key to all the mysteries, seeing as Abraham saw, all molecules, systems, universes. Seven represents diversity, the seven branches of the candlestick each of which contain a portion of the truth. Each of them possesses a part of the Adamic word of truth." He showed her the list he had made of seven groups of people in the valley.

"What is the word of truth of the Jews?" Jenny asked.

"Tradition. The Catholics' is ritual. Mormons', revelation. Polygamists', interpersonal relations. Scholars, abstractions. Businessmen, wealth. The seven archangels referred to in the book of Revelation are seven peoples or the words which stand for those people."

Jenny thought he was joking. "So who is the seventh sign?"

"We are. The five of us. With the one who will come. The six of us."

Jenny smiled. "And what is our core word?"

"Transmutation. We are changeable. When the end comes we will be transformed in the blinking of an eye." He looked at her. "I know it sounds crazy. But there are crazier things in the world, and the truth will always sound odd. What I'm looking for are the words Adam spoke, the pure language he learned from God. A language with no ambiguity, no possibility of duplicity. One word spoken in that language would transform the world, bring on the Apocalypse. Sometimes watching someone, I feel the word welling up inside me, the word which probably describes each of their essences. If we join all the words of all these essences, the world is born again."

"Too metaphysical for me," she said.

JENNY, CAPTURED BY THE MORMONS

"I used to feel the same dullness of mind."

"Pompous," she said. He shrugged his shoulders. Jenny had read Revelation herself, and it seemed to be what it professed to be, a hunted man writing beauty and peace in code. John was like her, adapting words so that they could be many things to many people. They both had to speak that way or they would die.

Peter said there was a word for every person. Of course that was true, every person had a word written on her heart, even Peter, every person was a puzzle until she understood the word. Peter's word was complex and many faceted, fluid and unstable. But the word of each person was obvious to Jenny, not something secret and sacred. Listening to Peter she understood again the most important idea of her life, that the creations of the imagination are indistinguishable from the creations of the senses.

"So how was work today?" she said.

He looked at her. "Don't be ironic. The harvest is white. That is my work."

She pictured a pale skinned woman, thirty-five, his second wife, enticed out of her tight Mormon virginity by his visions. "The harvest is white," she said.

"You're mocking me," he said. "But I don't mind it. You've known me long enough that you have no more reverence. A prophet in his own country."

A new development, when she thought he had hit bottom. A prophet now. He finished eating and pushed the plate back, watching her even more closely.

"You can sleep on the couch tonight," she said.

At first he was angry. "What is this?" Then his face was sad, he stared at his plate.

"You need to stay here or you need to leave. I won't be jerked back and forth anymore."

"Your manipulation won't work," he said. He brought blankets and rolled in them on the couch.

Jenny walked to the room where the children slept. She touched each one: Sariah, long of body, thin; Ruth, night-black hair; and Ishmael, whose mouth had fallen open. "He has an artist's lip," she whispered, an upward curve, parabolic.

Peter seemed to be asleep, and she sat near him, looking at his soft brush of black hair. Deceiving: actually his hair was coarse to the touch, strands thick as strings. He shampooed with something that smelled like apples—wherever he stayed, foolish man.

She had known a Texas boy, her first. Renegade son of a Muleshoe cotton farmer—thin, black-haired like Peter, sensuous as Mick Jagger. She tried to remember the swing of his shoulders and the lilt of his talk. "Honey," he had called her. "Your mouth tastes like honey." Sweet ol' sap. When he touched her, she became immediately moist. Light fingers.

Then he turned smug. I have the power to move you, his eyes said. I will own you entirely. Even at fifteen her shoulders had been heavy, her arms strong. She touched her hands to her breasts, belly, thighs. She thought of herself walking, free and straight, without affected dips and curves. Not afflicted with the disease of pleasing men. I am a solid woman. When he had turned smug, she thrust him away from her. It hurt as if she had taken a fist of flesh, pried loose a rib bone, and thrown it out. She sniffed, watching Peter. Thinking always made her weepy.

Peter slept like Ishmael, mouth half-open, teeth showing. She touched the lids of his large eyes, lids covered with tiny veins. Thick hair, tangled at the nape. She combed her fingers through his hair against the grain and then took a tuft in her teeth, tugging gently. Silly Jenny, she thought. You don't want him to wake. She put her face into his belly, blew softly as with a baby. Even now, except when he was in the throes of divinity, he was sensitive, nearly tremulous as a fawn. She had thought of that tentativeness as a strength—he had been wide-eyed, pure with joy, blooming every moment.

Sometimes he had yet another mood—a needy innocence which she didn't like. Be mama to me. I need another womb to crawl into. She felt dirty then. Sometimes he waked and moved her with his hand, his face luminous above her. Luxurious. All those moods were disappearing, swallowed up by his righteousness. She wished she could sob like a child.

She reached her hand to his hair, thick and wiry. "You always did have hog-bristle hair," Jenny said. He opened his eyes.

"If you sleep with a boar, what does that make you?" He smiled, his eyes full of pure physical desire, nothing insane. If only she could always wake him, bring him back.

"I'm the Mate of a Beast. Your nose looks like a hog nose."

"I think I have a refined nose." He snorted, then took her hand and nipped the fat part of her palm. She lunged backward from the couch, but he rolled, tangled in blanket, then chased her through the children's bedroom, trotting with knees high like a running back. He slipped on the rug in the hallway, and she was on him, straddling his belly and pinning him against the floor. She held him down, but he thrust his hands up between hers and began unbuttoning her shirt.

"Stop it," she said, then grinned. She would have him again. She wanted him sane, wanted him with her.

"I dreamed that we are going to have triplets."

"I couldn't survive that." She opened his shirt and buried her face in his belly, biting the roll there. He held his arms around her and twisted himself on top, kneeling, brushing his fingers outward on her neck, dry-lipping her neck and breasts. She reached for him, helped him remove his pants.

Before lying across her he placed his hands low on her belly, blessing her to conceive, and Jenny's desire faded away. She looked at his eyes, wondering that he was different so quickly, rough and vital, a clear open flame, then suddenly tight and visionary, a smoldering heat. She knew that it was a transformation only for her, that for him the praying and the play were one thing; she believed there was no difference of emotion or attitude from inside. But from her angle he crossed in and out, crossed and became uncer-

135

tain in thought and speech, so unsteady that she didn't know him, he didn't know himself, like a cold-blooded animal that can't recognize the danger in hot and cold. She would rather be a liar, feeling herself stable every instant.

"You need to purify your mind, body, and all the objects you touch," he said, "living in a state of Zion, like Enoch and his wives. I've had a revelation that Enoch possessed seven women." She had been right about him adopting polygamy as well as his other obsessions. "Only a test will determine if we are human or if we are worthy of being more than human and to join hand-in-hand with Christ when he returns bearing a sword which will spread flame from the East to the West," he said, still praying. His words were not really directed to God, they were more self-contained, like sentences in a manifesto.

The biggest joke was that his parents and all his Mormon relatives were as staid as clay: stable, conservative, middle-class farmers and businessmen. They thought that his fanaticism had sprouted instantly, like weed-contaminated seed spread in the night by an enemy. They abhorred him as if he possessed a devil, thought of his reversion to fundamentalism and mysticism as heretical. She understood it though. He had taken that which was latent in them, the oddness from a hundred years earlier, polygamy, mysticism, the darkness in every person, and had amplified it a hundredfold, becoming crazy. He thought he should have been born a hundred and thirty years earlier during the times of extremity of his own ancestors. Once he had even brought her a long dress with puffed sleeves, a pioneer dress, which he wanted her to wear before they had sex. She had refused and offended him.

Jenny remembered a street person she had met as she walked home with a loaf of bread she had lifted. He chased her, would have killed her for the bread. Pushed to the mental extreme, Peter might do anything unpredictable.

Peter's voice was thick but electric as if he spoke through a microphone. The Mouthpiece of God, she thought. Sometimes Peter was like a large mouth hung in the sky, talking and talking. Even God must get tired of listening. His weight on her, she couldn't move away and she held her breath. Damn, she thought, five minutes ago I wanted you. She felt the battle between his faith and the biochemical power of the contraceptive the welfare doctor had given her. Peter believed his dream, that he was engendering triplets. Jenny wondered what he would do if he discovered she had been using the devil's chemical.

On impulse she held the back of his neck, entwined her fingers in his stiff hair, and moved with him faster and faster. She tried not to think about the pills. Forty-six, forty-seven, forty-eight, she counted silently. Maybe that was one good thing about his fundamentalism, he endured to the end.

Could he read her mind?—one of God's idiot-savants who knew more than he could see, who knew more about her than she did herself? Her worry was keeping her from focusing on the pleasurable movement inside her. Instead of possessing extrasensory power, maybe Peter could sense her mental tension from the tightness of her loins. She had once read about a horse which seemed to read numbers from its owner's mind but in reality knew when and how often to raise a hoof because it perceived the minute motions and angles of its owner's body. Her body was like a sexual lie detector, infallible. She suddenly started giggling. Peter's regularity faltered. He raised himself on one arm, still filling her below, and held her face, his thumb on the line of her jaw, fingers on her throat. "What is it?" he said. "Tell me what you're thinking."

I'm not sure I want another child, she started to say—a half-lie; he would hear the whine in her voice and would start mistrusting her. The thought of another baby was despair, a forfeiture of control. "I don't want another child," she said. Not that she didn't need the three already born: their arms, legs, bellies separable inseparable of her flesh.

"You didn't say that." He began moving his hips again. As she looked up into his fanatical eyes, her thoughts stammered and the

137

hair rose on the back of her neck; she didn't know this man, her lover of five years. She would bring no more babies to such a man.

"Alleluia to God on high!" Peter shouted, and she knew he was finished.

Jenny lay awake, worried that he would rise and walk straight to the pills, his intuition released in his somnambulism.

She always hid them without thinking: once in the sugar jar, once buried in hamburger in the freezer, under their mattress where she felt their power working like a charm. But now time was running out; he would discover them in the bush and would be furious that his efforts at child-engendering were fruitless, that he was casting his precious seed into a ground which had been poisoned. If he didn't know from the lack of pregnancy, Peter would know from her lack of ardency in lovemaking.

For those children she had believed in the glory of conceiving and birthing; she had held him with her arms and legs, pulling him toward her with her fingers in his hair, teeth on his lips, holding him still inside afterward to make sure the little swimmers reached her belly. She felt the magnetic pull of them, rushing upward through her, as she was aware of insects and animals, up to where the egg lay ready. She had sensed it waiting inside her, three times.

What was a mother to a child? A father? Jenny's mama and daddy sang in a band, bluesy country music. He played the drums, she sang. Sitting in the garage on an old freezer, Jenny had been rocked by the bass, thick as gospel music. Oh, Lordy. Her mother's voice rang out even now. Her daddy was city librarian in the day—a thin, black-haired man, like her first lover, like Peter. At night he beat his drums. Her mama made wooden Noah's arks and sold them. Roughing out the small pieces by pushing them into an electric jigsaw, so intent that at least once every week she tipped her fingers and bled onto the animals and the metal base of the saw. She had a pencil-thin wood rasp, which she used to finish them. Jenny stuck a pin in their bellies and hung them from a string so she could paint finish on them, make them hard and brown.

Peter moved suddenly and left the bed, a darker shadow. She followed him to the girls' bedroom where he lifted Sariah. The child blinked awake, her body still limp.

"What are you doing?" asked Jenny.

"I feel inspired to bless them," he said as he settled Sariah into a chair where he lay his hands on her head. "I bless you that one day soon you will be transformed into what mortal eyes would see as a being of flame. In that condition you will be prepared for the Advent of God." The girl looked at Jenny, waiting quietly until her father was finished. Peter had never gone this far before—waking the children in the middle of the night. Jenny forced her own face quiet in order to reassure her daughter.

He prayed over the others, lifting Ruth into the chair, then making Jenny sit with Ishmael in her arms. "Father, Son, and Holy Ghost," he called the three children, his sense of patriarchy so strong that he forgot that two of her children were females. Something like a sex change operation, thought Jenny, making a way for her anger to wait. He should say Mother, Daughter, and Holy Ghost. "All of these will be translated in the blinking of an eye. Their brief mortal existence will have earned them everlasting glory."

"Let them go back to bed," she said as calmly as she could.

Peter still prayed over Ishmael. "It's time for the resurrection of the just, time for the battle between the Son and the Anti-Christ. Soon you will be tested to determine whether you are divine or merely human. If you are not human, your clothing will burn away as you fall and a trump will sound. Through you destruction will be poured out on a sinful world."

Jenny was shaking with fear and anger as she settled the children back to sleep. It's time for us to leave, she thought. Our luck has run out.

III

Two hours before dawn Peter woke her. Not a morning person, Jenny forced herself to the stove and turned on the burner under the pot of cracked-wheat mush, pioneer food, she had set soaking the evening before. Peter waited for his breakfast at the table — turned inside himself again. He was probably considering whether he had stamina to visit another of his wives before returning to her that night. Planting each field in turn, hoping for at least one crop of immortals.

After eating he moved to the door. "Back after dark. Don't stop taking the herbs with your food, they'll keep your clock accurate." He moved quickly down the street so that the neighbors wouldn't see him. He reached with one leg then drew the other up quickly, so he appeared to run sideways. "The way he thinks," she murmured. With him out of the house, she could breathe again.

She had five options which arrayed themselves in her mind: (1) Cynthia, the welfare woman — an unlikely prospect; (2) the woman at planned parenthood, who, fascinated by the quandary of the wife of a reactionary fundamentalist taking birth control, had slipped her some food money — wouldn't work twice; (3) the people at the Salt Sea Mission of Hope — not enough time with nothing but a flier to go on; (4) working downtown again — the best so far, but she wasn't sure she had time and patience to find a sitter and then to work up the level of believable pain, especially since her anxiety to be gone would manifest itself; (5) the Mormon Relief Society president. "May she give me relief," Jenny said, her decision made, her voice droning like a chant. She recognized an expansion inside — hope, like being in love, only now the swelling was anticipatory of being free of Peter.

Ishmael stirred and she took him up, lifted her breast to his lips. Later they drowsed together, his mouth half opened on her thickened nipple, milk on his mouth. Rising she laid him in the drawer which was his crib and stuffed herself back in her shirt, hooking the flap of her bra. The children would be an asset with the Relief Society president.

140   She carried Ishmael slung in front of her; the two girls walked beside. They walked in sunlight, having left later than the day before, so that the light had already descended across the western lake to the church office building and the temple. Peter couldn't look at the gray spires without anger. "They don't think I'm pure enough to enter," he said. You apostatized, she thought, you believe in what they abandoned a century ago.

Jenny knocked on the door of the president's house, a woman in charge of the physical and spiritual welfare of the women in her congregation. The door opened, but Jenny stood without talking or moving.

"Jenny," said Sister Johnson. "Jenny, what's wrong?"

"Can I come in?"

"Of course." She pulled them in, her arms around Jenny's shoulders. Jenny shifted the baby to clasp her hand on Sister Johnson's arm and shoulder. Mormons were always hugging or shaking hands.

Jenny looked down, studying the other woman; she was four inches shorter than Jenny, compact, dark-haired, with a vital face. When Sister Johnson entered the Relief Society room, she was like a presence, quietly controlling everyone, a short Wonder Woman, teaching the ladies, guiding them in Compassionate Service projects. Jenny wouldn't have been surprised if Sister Johnson had taken out an iron frying pan and bent it double.

"Your children look good," she said, waiting. Jenny noticed bread dough on Sister Johnson's hands, watched her inner clock ticking. Charts on the refrigerator: this child does dishes this day, each act of the day precisely ordered. Don't begrudge her, Jenny thought, just a different way of thinking about time, trapped in sixty compartments a minute, efficient; she does want to help if I move carefully and quickly.

"It's a miracle they do."

"What's wrong with them?"

Jenny examined the other woman's face, waiting until she sensed the right words. But in this case the right words would be the wrong ones. Jenny knew that Sister Johnson wouldn't help someone who was clear and cogent.

"Nothing's wrong with them." Jenny looked at her own hands. Sister Johnson waited as well, but Jenny needed her to talk. "They can feel it even when we try to hide it from them." She saw doubt in Sister Johnson's eyes—drawing sympathy for children must have been used on her before.

"Just tell me what's happened."

Jenny knew she needed to be more direct. "My husband has left me."

"I thought he left some time ago."

"He has been going then coming back. He has been coming home about once a week."

"Have you talked to the bishop?"

"I wanted to talk to you first. I didn't know what he would say. I thought he might blame me."

"I thought you said before that your husband was completely gone."

"He wasn't helping me, and I didn't think you would help me either if I told you he was half gone." Nothing was right. Jenny felt sweat start on her forehead.

Sister Johnson's eyes were wary, wary. Too many beggars had tricked her, a class of people even more transient than Jenny, moving from ward to ward milking Church Welfare. Jenny had talked to some of them who were asked by the bishop to help clean her house and yard in return for welfare commodities. "Have you talked to your home teachers?" Sister Johnson said. The men who visited every month, a network informing the bishop and this woman, like spies.

"I don't know who is assigned to me."

"They've never come?" Sister Johnson's mouth tightened. Finally Jenny had the right-wrong angle.

"They came once a long time ago."

"Visiting teachers?"

Jenny shrugged her shoulders.

"I wish I could trust them," said Sister Johnson. "What is your husband doing?"

"I don't know. He's gone now. I haven't seen him for a month."

"What have you been living on?"

Jenny saw that the woman would give her food. Remembering her weakness when Peter's mind moved back to the nineteenth century, she said suddenly, "I think he's gone crazy. I look in his eyes and I think that he's going to beat me. His eyes are crazy. My husband is crazy."

"I thought you said he was gone."

"I'm frightened that he will come back. That's why I came to talk to you. He'd shout at night because he thought someone was after him. When he was awake he thought the same thing. So he finally just left our home." Home. A nice round word, worshipped by the woman before her. Happy home. Happiness is Family Home Evening.

Watching Sister Johnson's face, Jenny knew she might have ruined it; she would have to divide her words even more carefully. "Praise the Lord," started to come out, a mistake, a tick like a drug flashback from her time in Muleshoe with her Baptist father. She hadn't been there for twenty years, the words so buried she didn't know if she could drag them out. The wrong language. The glory of God is a burnin' inside. Translate it. "I could feel the presence of the Holy Ghost, protecting me before he left." The right words were still wrong, tangled even to her. She had let Peter get to her mind; he had upset her confidence. "I'm punished for my sins, I know it," Jenny said.

"Of course not," said the woman. "Don't be ridiculous."

"I once knew a woman whose three children were taken from her by God because she wouldn't obey his commandment to speak his credit in all things. When her husband left, she wouldn't say the Lord's will be done, she said, the devil take him. When she lost her house she said the Lord taketh and the Lord taketh again, no men-

143

tion of any of the giving He had done. While she was out working one day, her house burned down. Electrical fire, said the fireman, she didn't dare tell him that her electricity had been disconnected and that there was no possibility of an electrical fire."

Sister Johnson's face still showed confusion, and Jenny had forgotten how to use it. "You really think that?"

Jenny said nothing, again watching Sister Johnson's face, she knew that, despite her confusion, it was finally all right, an arbitrary stroke of luck.

"I can give you food. I can give you another order."

Jenny needed money today. "If the starter were fixed on my car I could go look for a job."

"Will Sister Parker watch your children?"

"Yes. I mean, I don't know. She's helped me too much already."

Sister Johnson frowned. "I want you to work for this order. You've received food for six months now and it's time you earned some of it. I have three or four women, older sisters, who can do none of their own cleaning. I want you to clean Sister Frank's house today."

Jenny wondered if she could ask to do the work later. Probably not. She didn't mind working, but she didn't have time today. Today she needed to be on the road. "You do need food?" Sister Johnson was prodding after the pause. The statement angered her because it marked Sister Johnson's authority as a keeper of the keys. Only through me can you get food for your children.

"Yes," said Jenny. "I will be happy to work for it."

"You need something else?"

"Just money for the starter."

"We can talk about that after you're finished. Have you been looking for work?"

"Yes," Jenny said angrily. "I can't get a job where I can take care of them."

144

"I wasn't suggesting anything."

"Can I get the order now?" Jenny thought she could sell some of the food.

Sister Johnson smiled. "You need to do the work first. You can get the order filled on Thursday when the store is open."

"You're not going to give me any food?"

"I didn't say that. I can on Thursday."

"You can in an emergency. We're out of food today." Jenny let her anger go.

"Are you out of food? Is this an emergency?"

"You don't know what it is. You sit in this big house and you wait for your husband to come home. He's working for you. You don't know what it's like."

"I just want you to feel the capacity to do for yourself if your husband won't."

"What do you mean, the capacity to do? What should I do?"

"You should wash windows today."

"Now why in God's name would I want to do that?" Jenny said. "You can't know what my life is like? You can't know. I need it today. I haven't got any food. I can't wait for it. I'll go steal something."

"You go wash this woman's windows, I'll give you a food order when you come back. You can get it today."

Damn, thought Jenny, I'm losing it.

At home Jenny called the auto shop and asked how much a starter motor would cost.

"Sixty-five with exchange," he said.

"Do you have any arrangements for credit?"

"Sorry ma'am." She heard him slap his book shut.

Any day she could earn seventy dollars. Jenny decided she had to try working downtown. She walked with the children toward Sister Parker's but remembered it was Saturday. The woman would watch no children that day. Jenny had tried before. Begging wouldn't work with children and it wouldn't work on a Saturday and she didn't have time. She shouldn't have spent all the money on food.

145

Moving slowly with her children, Jenny walked ten blocks south, almost to Liberty Park, to Lily White Used Cars. The logo was a bride dressed in lace.

"I want a car for under a thousand." If she asked for something more, he wouldn't trust her. They walked down the rows of cars: a Ford LTD station wagon, the edge of the underbody rusted out, no price written on the window (if you have to ask you can't afford it); a little Toyota truck, front left fender crumpled; a Chevrolet Impala, repainted puce; a GMC pick-up, a plastic hand flipping the bird in place of the shifter knob; a Buick Skylark, lemon yellow, black interior, the paint peeling. She lifted the hood and peered at the engine, burnt black with oil. "Where're the keys?" While he walked to the building for them, she looked underneath at the drive shaft, which was bent where someone had run over a curb or something. "The drive shaft is crooked," she said when he returned. "Let me see the LTD."

She started the engine and heard a valve lifter clicking. The odometer said forty thousand. A hundred and. Tires were wearing uneven on the front. None of the others in the lot would be any better. "Can I drive it around the block?" She held the door open for the kids, then offered her driver's license to him. He didn't take it.

"New policy," he said. "I need to ride with you." New policy of the minute, Jenny thought. It was having the kids with her, but she hadn't dared leave them playing in the park. Someone like Peter, only twisted in the opposite direction, might come along. She drove the long-bodied car up Seventh East and turned at the first block. On the side street she accelerated to thirty, then slammed on the brakes. His bald head bobbed forward, and she wished she was strong and quick enough to push him out the door with her feet.

"Let me try the Jimmy."

He placed a small paper bag over the shifter. "Glued on," he said. "I haven't had time to hack-saw it off."

He drove around with her in two other cars. "Aren't you afraid you'll lose customers?" she said on their last go round.

"It's a policy. I don't make policy."

She walked off the lot with her children. They rode the bus to another dealer, but after seeing how he looked at the kids she didn't even try to get in a car.

Because Jenny didn't have any more for bus fare, they walked back. Ruth started crying and so Jenny lifted her to one hip. Her back ached, and she had wanted to be gone before Peter returned. Her thoughts flicked from plan to plan, all foolish ones: she couldn't work under this kind of pressure.

They cut across a Safeway parking lot; Sariah walked with one hand hooked in Jenny's back pocket. The cars were in rows, not uniform as they were in new car lots. Someone might rush into the store for bread or milk, forgetting the keys. She peered in window after window.

"I can't remember where I parked it," she said to a bagger who came out to retrieve carts. He stood and watched until she left. Six more blocks was a Smith's. She discovered no prospects at first, then found a car with the keys locked inside. She walked through the store to the bathroom, finding where the employees kept their jackets on wire hangers. Outside again, she fished inside the door until a police car pulled onto the lot. A man who had been standing in front of the store bent to talk to the officer. The man pointed toward where Jenny worked on the car; then he stood and shielded his eyes. She slid the hanger out and walked away slowly.

At Liberty Park she sat on a bench. The girls lay in the grass, not interested in the swings a short distance away.

Peter had prophesied that when Ishmael was thirteen the war between Gog and Magog would be unleashed on the world. He and she had once hiked to the top of Butterfield Pass and with a borrowed telescope had looked down on the two military installations in the adjacent valleys, storage places for bombs and poison gas. "There's another one just out of our sight—all instruments of

147

God, bringing the Apocalypse." She thought about the possibility of firestorms when her son turned thirteen.

She panicked and walked with Sariah and Ruth toward the center of the park, where she tried to beg. People avoided her, eyes on her children. Finally Jenny dragged the two girls back to her apartment, surprised that they weren't crying. She dressed herself in the clothing she had used to work downtown, finding rags and ammonia and went with the children to wash Sister Frank's windows. Afterward Jenny returned to Sister Johnson's house. "I've done the work," she said.

"I know. Sister Frank called to thank me." Sister Johnson gave her a requisition for food.

"I'd like to get my starter fixed today if I could."

"Tomorrow we can get the bishop to sign a check. He's gone with his family for the weekend and I need to talk to him about it." Jenny left without arguing.

She returned to her house and lay the useless food order on the table. She stood thinking, then she gathered cleaning equipment together in a white bucket and walked toward the foothills. With the children behind her she went from door to door. "Clean your house for twenty dollars," she said when they answered. Each woman looked at her children behind her and made some excuse, as Jenny knew they would. She tried each door where no one answered. Finally finding one unlocked, she walked inside to where the keys hung in the kitchen. She backed the car, an Audi, out of the garage and loaded the kids. She parked it five blocks away from her apartment and ran to her car, removing her license plates. Running back to the Audi, she replaced its plates with her own and drove away. Suddenly she stopped and climbed out, unbolting the plates and walking quickly away from it with her children. Driving it was waving a flag. Every policeman in three states would be looking for such a car.

At the door of the bishop's storehouse, a man loaded food into the back of a pickup. "Thirteen families will eat tonight: 13, 30, 7,

2730 families in Salt Lake City will eat this month. Can you comprehend the condescension of God?"

Sister Johnson, who had driven her, marched into the building. Jenny and the children followed. "You get these," she said, gesturing at the order, "and I'll get the supplies you need to make bread." Jenny walked through the store loading the food: peanut butter, corn syrup, raisins, butter, cans of meat.

While Sister Johnson lectured on the merits of home-made bread, Jenny numbered the hours until Peter would come—three, four at the most. On Seventh East was a house where a woman bought welfare food at half price. She provided a service for people who wanted to use food stamps or bishop's order forms to get beer and cigarettes. Jenny stacked the food on Sariah's wagon and made her walk alongside to balance the load while Jenny pulled it, the baby strapped to her chest. She got forty dollars for her order, not enough. She pulled the children in the wagon, running back to her house. Then she quickly took the starter out of her car, loaded it and her children onto the bus, and rode to North Salt Lake where there was a junk yard. The owner had arranged starters on a shelf. After a few minutes of looking she found one which matched. She left the old one for him to rebuild. "This is a good starter," he said to her. "Guaranteed. That's thirty bucks."

Stupid, stupid, stupid, she thought as she rode the bus. Anyone else would have stolen a car by now. She didn't trust Peter to stay away until an hour after dark.

Underneath the car she could see nothing: the light was failing. She felt the three children moving in the car above her. She reached down near her hip and pulled the starter motor, which scraped heavily across the cement. "Sariah," she called, "can you shine the light for me?"

The girl opened the door and flashed the light haphazardly under the car. "Here," Jenny said. "Flash it here." She lifted the starter motor and pushed it upwards into the darkness. He would come in half an hour. She twisted the body of the starter so that it wouldn't

149

fall out and reached for the bolts. When she tried to slide the starter into place, it slipped, dropping onto her chest, tumbling down next to her armpit. Cramped in the tight space, she couldn't reach it with either hand. She slid over and bent her elbow, but then she didn't have the strength to lift the motor. She lay resting in the cool darkness; she had no other way to leave the city.

Pushing herself part way out, she reached both hands above her head and thrust the starter upward. When it was up inside the belly of the car, she could balance it with one hand. She reached with her free hand back behind her head for the bolt, feeling it under her shoulder. She touched the hole with her finger, lifting and twisting the starter with her other hand, turning the bolt until it caught. She used the wrench on it, turning, finding the bolt with her fingers then sliding the wrench into place, frantically turning it. "Slow, slow," she said. "You'll strip it."

She slid out from under the car and lifted herself, one hand on the door, pushing herself upward. Opening the hood, she reached down into the engine and cut her arm on something sharp. She didn't jerk her hand out. Instead she found the hole and twisted the bolt, which turned and turned without catching. She leaned forward against the car, knowing she would have to get back under and loosen the lower bolt so that she could get the upper one to catch.

She rushed under the car and loosened the lower bolt, then shoved herself out and up again, turning the upper bolt, then shifting the motor and turning the bolt again until she felt it catch. After she tightened it as far as she could with her fingers, she fitted the wrench on, but there wasn't enough room to do more than a half an inch turn. She flipped the wrench back and forth, moving the bolt a fraction each time. Patience. A hundred small motions to get it tight. " . . . down on me." She whispered Janis Joplin to keep her mind functioning. The children sat in the car, quiet now that it was completely dark.

She crawled back under the car and tightened the lower bolt

all the way. Touching the end of the starter with her fingers, she found the brass extension where the cable attached. She fastened it and the smaller solenoid wire; then she slid out and jumped inside, grease on her hands. Nothing happened when she turned the key. The battery cables weren't attached. She jerked the door open and ran forward, quickly sliding them on without tightening. The engine ground and ground as she pumped the gas. Finally it caught and started.

She rushed through the house, grabbing clothing and belongings, stuffing them into a suitcase. She lugged it outside and met Peter in the driveway. He opened his hand and showed her the plastic package of contraceptives. "These are yours," he said. "I know it."

IV

"I've been watching from behind the dumpster," Peter said. "You're trying to leave me." He sounded as if he couldn't believe it. "You're trying to abandon your own eternal glory."

He reached for her arm as she pushed the suitcase through the window of the car, but she pulled back.

"Don't touch me," she said. "I *will* damn well hurt you if you touch me." She squared herself in front of him and glared into his face until he believed her.

"I don't want it to come to that," he said. He turned and went inside the house. She could leave then, gathering the children; maybe he would just let her go. Instead she followed him inside. He sat on the couch, his fists between his knees.

She washed her hands in the kitchen then returned to the living room. The package of pills lay on the arm of the couch; she took them back.

"You don't need those," he said.

"I may," she said.

"You have no respect for me or for your body." She saw that he was angry and shocked; leaving didn't bother him as much as taking back the pills. She filled her denim bag with clothing.

"I need you to come with me for an hour," Peter said. "Then I'll let you go to your damnation. I'll not force you to stay."

"Why?"

"I need you to understand something. Leave the kids asleep."

"I won't leave them."

"We'll be gone fifteen minutes."

"I told you I won't leave them." Jenny continued packing. She tried to estimate how much she could trust him. He stood and sidled across the room, one foot behind the other, his old walk. He rippled like a slow image in the movies, multiple exposures. Stopping in front of her, he put one hand to his forehead as he did when he was anxious. So much of him remained. She wanted to remember each motion and gesture after she was gone.

"I've decided that I'll stop you from going, and if you somehow get away, I'll report it that you've stolen my car." Disoriented, she stared at him. "Even if they believe you, they'll still bring you back to talk about it." He knew she had left her driver's license in her own name. "If you come with me now, and you don't change your mind about leaving, I won't try to keep you."

His mind was soup, but he had never lied to her. She believed that going with him was the easiest way to become disentangled. Next door lived a single father and his children. The children slept alone while he worked every night. Jenny walked down the hall, through their front door, always unlocked, and into the bedroom of the middle child, a boy of twelve. He woke partway, losing his fear when he recognized her face.

"Watch my children," Jenny spoke sharply in his ear, pulling him half out of bed, breathing him awake. "Keep them safe until I come back and I'll pay you ten dollars." The boy's eyes popped open, and he followed her through his dark living room.

At ten o'clock Jenny drove Peter downtown. He sat in the passenger seat, sullen, pointing in advance of each turn. He directed her left as they reached the Mormon office building, tallest in Salt Lake City. "Park here," he said. The dark, steep street led from the corner of the building up to the state capitol, green-roofed from the polluted air which transformed the copper. Jenny breathed the taint of smog in the air. The lights of the city rose below her, growing fainter, like mist rising from swamp-ground. The office building towered across from them, large, square, brightly lit. If she and Peter had walked on air they could have entered the fifth floor windows. Next to the office building stood the gray, many-spired temple. She had tried working the lobby of the office building once, which was as large as an ice skating rink, but the security guards had moved her out.

She didn't ask Peter to explain himself as they walked closer; she wanted to wait and watch. Each side of the large white facade had a globe of the world in bas-relief. Two white worlds—eastern and western hemispheres. She looked up at the glowing building framed by the night sky. The white room inside black curtains, reverse of the Jack Bruce song. Peter hated the Mormon leaders, said they had tried to transform eternal truth. She wondered what he was doing. He might try to make her help burn the building, destroy the property of people he considered foreigners and enemies. She turned her mind from Peter's possible violence to her memory of Jack Bruce's voice, which rose inside her, a talisman. Peter glanced over his shoulder at her, leading her without telling her some mystery, happy in her bewilderment. His eyes were still crazy, but she remembered that formerly his glance had melted her bones. "Silver horses climb down moonbeams in your dark eyes." Jack Bruce's silky voice descended a tonal ladder as Peter led Jenny into the lobby.

He put one hand on Jenny's shoulder, pushing her slightly forward. "Trainee," he said to the two security guards seated behind a panel of steady green lights. They smiled and nodded, knowing him, then turned back to their monitors. Someone else came in behind them, dressed in levis and white shirt, a young man, as innocent faced as the Baptist with the pamphlets. Peter smiled and nodded and led her by the arm to the banks of elevators, up to the third

153

floor; the other young man remained. She watched the number above the door mark the elevator's passage upward: 12, 13, 14.

Jenny was suddenly weary after all the rushing that day. The halls were long, dark, empty. Peter punched the buttons on a wall phone and the halls lit. He opened a door and trundled a wheeled garbage can out. He opened door after door along the hallway, removing the trash. A beeping sounded as he opened each door, a chorus of electronic crickets: warning, warning.

"Come here," he said. She walked closer. "That sound is an alarm. They know it's me, so they don't pay any attention. See I've learned something from you." The noise continued, pulse and pulse. Still holding the can, Peter turned to stare into her face.

"How long?" she said. It was all she could do to keep from laughing at his subterfuge.

"Eleven months." Peter grinned at her. "We've all had our secrets." He made it a pronouncement, as if working as a janitor was an essential infiltration. "And no one knows what I am."

He opened doors and shut them, sometimes dumping trash sometimes simply opening and shutting doors in haphazard fashion. Jenny imagined red-lights blinking on the panel below, hypnotic, marking opening and shutting of doors. Peter made the lights invisible.

In the east wing he led her into the musty stacks of books. He walked down the aisle, pushing his broom in front of him. Then he lifted a book and read it, sitting cross legged on the floor. "Rare books," he said. "This is the only way I could get access to them. They contain the abandoned mysteries of God. Listen: 'Men on Kolob walk like angels, beings whose intelligence has transformed their bodies into fire and light.'"

After a time he walked to the back. He opened a door and shut it, waiting, then he opened the door again, more noise. He pulled from his pocket a wire which had magnets attached to each end. He fastened the wire to the door and the door frame and the noise stopped as if the door had opened and shut again. "Rarest of the rare. I've thought many times about burning this room. They would have to notice and change then." He lifted a phone, pressed the buttons. The lights went out. "All done," he said to the air.

"When you remove that, they'll know you were in here."

"Or that I returned. These books trace the changes. You wouldn't believe all the ways they've changed the church," he said. "God wouldn't reveal something and then contradict himself."

She heard him moving in the darkness. The books smelled a thousand years old. Peter's face appeared suddenly, illuminated by a pocket light. He sat on the floor reading. Soon he kneeled and prayed. "When, Lord? I've been patient, Lord, waiting your pleasure. I pray that the time is now. I know that you're waiting for the ripening of conditions, but I also know that you have the power to transform conditions. I believe and pray that it is now."

She watched him in the dim light, mourning what had been lost, unhappy that his mad voice made the hair rise on the back of her neck. Once on a farm near Muleshoe a dog had circled her, not barking, grinning, almost as a human would grin, circling ten feet away, trying to get behind her. She had dipped quickly for a stick and circled with him, moving slowly toward a woven-wire fence.

Peter stopped praying and stood, the light dangling at his side. His white-rimmed, staring eyes were more alien than the dog's impossible smile. "My research is finished," he said to Jenny. "It's time for the purging to begin. Falling from the top of this building, a divine being would be transformed from flesh to light and flame. You need to return here with the children. A test to make sure they are divine. It is your only possibility for redemption." On the top of the building was an observation deck, protected by cement walls and woven wire.

She rose from the floor and shut the door to the archives behind her, running toward the elevator. She heard him, felt him grip her arm, spinning her around. "You were almost persuaded once," he said. "We two could have been archangels to the highest." He wouldn't let her go. She readied her knee. But then he relaxed and

155

moved backward from her, smiling, his teeth showing. Jenny walked backward, watching him, moving slowly so she wouldn't alarm him, just as she had with the dog.

Once around the corner she slapped her open hand again and again on the elevator button. The doors opened, and Peter turned the corner, head lowered. She punched the button and the door shut; the elevator went down. She knew Peter would follow her, so as soon as the door opened, she sprinted across the foyer toward the security desk. She heard his footsteps, but then the sound stopped. When she turned, he was standing in front of the express elevator to the main tower. The doors opened and he disappeared inside.

She rushed up to the two officers. "Peter's crazy," she shouted at them. "He's going to jump." The two hesitated, looking at each other then back at her. "He's going to jump off the observation deck," she said slowly. "And I'm going to count every second before you move. You better damn well believe the newspapers are going to know to the second how long it took you to move. He's going to jump you stupid fools."

They moved. One flipped a switch and a ringing began at the elevators. He ran toward the sound. The other called security higher in the building. The same one was talking to the police as Jenny backed away from the desk and moved out the wide front doors. She ran to her car and drove to the west side of the building, where the observation deck extended to the edge. Five police cars, a fire truck, and an ambulance arrived in ten minutes. She left fifteen minutes later, when she was sure they had him.

"We're going on a night trip," she said to Sariah. "Help Ruth get her blanket into the car." She sent the neighbor boy home with all her money, a little over six dollars. "I'm sorry, it's all I've got." Sariah and Ruth walked out of their room, wide-eyed because of excitement in the middle of the night. Jenny carried the baby.

At the edge of the city she picked up an eighteen-year-old boy. He had thirty dollars, which he said she could use to buy gas, and he was running from Denver to California. She sang John Mayall to him. "I can't do my best unless I've got room to move." His face was hard, no innocence, and she loved him suddenly. In California she would watch her children's eyes and the motions and equations of their bodies as they grew, determining for herself whether they were human.

She drove west around the lake toward the Salt Flats and Nevada. The boy pretended to sleep, watching her through slits of lids, down then up, eyes moving across her body in minute twitches. As she approached the tall, white stacks at Kennecott, she imagined Peter falling in the city behind her, still falling, and she waited for the burst of light, like an atomic flash, which would spread toward her across the lake.